108
H25r

83514

DATE DUE			
Jul 2 '73			
Jul 9 '73			
May 19 '75			
Mar 10 '76			
Feb 28 7g			
Mar 21 79			

Reality as Social Process

STUDIES IN METAPHYSICS AND RELIGION

Reality As Social Process

STUDIES IN METAPHYSICS AND RELIGION

BY CHARLES HARTSHORNE

UNIVERSITY OF CHICAGO

FOREWORD BY WILLIAM ERNEST HOCKING

Reprint with Corrections of the 1953 Edition

HAFNER PUBLISHING COMPANY
New York
1971

CONTENTS

ACKNOWLEDGMENTS

For kind permission to republish articles (in somewhat altered form) acknowledgment is due the following publications:

The Hibbert Journal for Chapter 1, originally published under the title, "A New Philosophical Conception of the Universe": LIV (1945), no. 1.

Comment (University of Chicago student literary quarterly) for Chapter 2, originally published under the title, "Pattern and Movement in Art and Science": III (1935), no. 2.

Social Research for Chapter 3: IX (1942), no. 2.

Theoria: A Swedish Journal of Philosophy and Psychology for Chapter 4: XV (1949), no. 1.

The Philosophical Review for Chapter 5: LVIII (1949), no. 5; Chapter 6: LV (1946), no. 2.

The Journal of Religion for Chapter 7: XXVI (1946), no. 3.

Journal of Liberal Religion for Chapter 8: VIII (1946), no. 1; Chapter 9: I (1940), no. 3.

Journal of Bible and Religion for Chapter 10: XVI (1948), no. 1.

The University Review (Kansas City) for Chapter 11: III (1937), no. 4.

The Christian Century for Chapter 12: LVII (1940), no. 10. (Review of *The Philosophy of John Dewey*.)

Journal of Religion for Chapter 13: XXV (1945), no. 4. (Review of *The Philosophy of Bertrand Russell.*)

Ethics for the first two paragraphs of Chapter 14: LIII (1943), no. 3.

FOREWORD

To those who doubt whether there is progress in philosophy, it may be pointed out that in the three hundred years since Descartes died philosophical mankind has learned something. The word Descartes is not equivalent to the word modernity, yet no other figure so symbolizes the spirit of modern thought: a broad departure from Cartesian theses and assumptions implies an inner development of modern philosophy, a critique of modernity itself, and the readiness of this moment for a new stage of fundamental construction.

There is a near consensus—as near as philosophers ought ever to achieve—over some of Descartes' theses: for example that we can no longer accept the clean split between mind and body, which as a working hypothesis set laboratory science free for methodological cleanliness and a triumphant sweep of theory; nor the bisection of our physical experience into the sense-qualities which are subjective and the quantities which are "out there" and "real"; nor the precise mathematical perfection of every detail of physical sequence, inside and outside of organic bodies. These items of conventional Cartesianism are not false—we still use them. It is simply that they are not "the truth," and that we cannot tell the truth now available to us in terms of the space, time, masses, and laws of formula of Galileo or Newton, of Lavoisier or Laplace, or Helmholtz or Tyndall, or even of Clerk-Maxwell. We require new concepts for physics, but also for the world at large new categories.

One feature, however, of Cartesian thinking we are not discarding, and I am not sure it isn't the chief mark of the modern era. I venture to say we shall never discard it. It is the inseparability of science and philosophy, of physics and metaphysics. Every future philosophic era will be, like our

[11]

modern era, for better or for worse "scientific" in the sense that whatever science reveals belongs integrally to the philosophical world picture. But the era now opening has the special task of putting science into its place.

This implies that science is not the whole of truth nor scientific method the whole of human thinking. As laboring to weld together the sciences with philosophy, our pragmatists, naturalists, realists and positivists have labored well. But to put science into its place requires a *pou sto* beyond science: that is the task of metaphysics. The era on which we are entering is marked by nothing so much as by a revival of metaphysical courage—the will not merely to observe and describe, but to understand. The standpoint we have now earned, or recovered after many vicissitudes, is the rational possession of the natural faith that reason is not given to man in order that it shall be frustrated. The audacious dialectic of Kant's *Critique of Pure Reason* has stood for nigh two centuries as a monument of muscular intellectual self-surrender—the work of a giant binding man's thought of the Whole in chains of insoluble paradox. This proud humility has been congenial to the scientific age just past: the time has now come to undo these chains, and with equal strength and greater clarity to move beyond the Kantian position.

It is true that a genuine moving-beyond was done in the period following Kant by the great line of German idealism, but it was done at the intolerable cost of breaking liaison with science. Only Fechner, the physicist, caught, in 1879, the full measure of the problem and became for a brief moment physicist, psychologist and metaphysician. Philosophy in America has in later years followed a more auspicious course for the present requirements. Since Charles Peirce, American thought has maintained its scientific rapport and intelligence: John Dewey, William James, Josiah Royce were all in various ways close students of science and of the logic of the sciences. And from their hands sprang that brief but vigorous period of constructive cosmology which deserves to be called the period of The Builders from roughly 1880 to 1920.

It is my private conviction that Dewey has for years been a metaphysician in disguise—a disguise which has cost him increasing feats of ingenuity, and which, for an instant, slipped aside in his remarkable "A Common Faith." Be this as it may, into our period of building intruded, at the turn of the century, a series of waves of criticism—the realisms, positivisms, semanticisms—to which we gave heed with less than due appreciation of the fact that the power of logical analysis, in even finer subtlety, was already a part of our inheritance. Charles Peirce had made Royce possible, and had paved the way for the adequate reception in America of the epochal work of Whitehead. To our careful and patient editors of Peirce's work, especially to Hartshorne and Weiss, all later American philosophy owes a lasting debt.

We have no reason to deplore these intermediate years of wandering in the wilderness, the anti-metaphysical tool-sharpening years, during which logical positivism has shot its bolt. If a negative analysis has gained a wide hearing it is because the work of The Builders has been less than cogent. If they, the analysts, were right in condemning philosophical construction, we should be obliged to them for sparing mankind fruitless labor and empty altercation. If they are wrong, we may still be obliged to them for compelling the work of thought to proceed on sounder and more persuasive footing. Philosophy has always made its strongest advances when it has listened respectfully to the skeptics, as Kant listened to Hume.

Professor Hartshorne has, on principle, listened respectfully to the skeptics. He has made his own the treasures of German speculation—and it is folly to suppose that the advance of philosophy can bypass that high point of spiritual enthusiasm, whatever its excesses and later humiliation—but he has equally made his own the main positions of the scientific and logical pioneering of this century. Peirce and Whitehead have been his companions. He has wrestled with the problems of paradox and dialectic as they appear not alone in the tradition of metaphysics and theology, but as they pervade the struggles of mankind to attain clarity about ultimate problems. He has come out with an affirmative faith in the calling of reason in our generation: he is again a Builder, but on the new foundations.

In an age which is disposed to give "the irrational" a large place, perhaps the dominating place, in human destiny as well as in the processes of the human will, he has made it his cause to do battle for the necessity of rational consistency in our thinking, and for the equal necessity that this thinking shall not shirk the metaphysical issues. This necessity lies upon us, whether in war or in peace; but in catastrophic times, it is particularly pertinent to remember that the great issues of public life are at root also metaphysical issues. And if this necessity lies upon us, there must be a possibility of success.

But there is another correction—to my mind the chief correction—which the assumptions of Descartes and of most of modernity after him require.

It is not in the field of science, nor in the world-deep entwinement of mind and matter. It is in the pivot of Descartes' reasoning, the radical and simple formula for his own ultimate certitude (which by a miracle of unrecognized assumption he interpreted as everyman's ultimate certitude), the "I think: I exist." Without feeling the searching force of this probing identity no one can enter modern philosophy; if it is taken as final, no one can escape from 'modernity.' Through three hundred years this formula has had a stream of critics; but the definitive escape is the deed, I am inclined to say the necessary deed, of the present century.

Already in my student days at the very opening of the century there were rumors of a breach in the egocentric enclosure of individual selfhood. Ralph Perry had recognized the "predicament" and had denounced the current reasoning based on it. Royce and James were quoting Baldwin's psychological studies of a "social factor" in the growth of the child's mind. They, Royce and James, seemed to me to be blurring the identity (and responsibility) of the "I think" through trying to intrude into it an indefinite and fuzzy "we think." The word "factor" struck me as an illicit metaphor from the physical picture of vector-addition. Yet in this direction there was something of first-rate importance. For after all, the "I think" is an incomplete statement. No one is ever "just thinking": he is always thinking *something*—always *je pense quelque chose, cogito aliquid.*

And indeed, this *aliquid* is essential to the meaning of the

"I" that thinks. It is an infinitery variable entity whereas the thinker is a constant; but there always is an *aliquid,* distinguishable from the "I"; and my identity as a self is known to me through being always other than this *aliquid,* other-than-the-other. Self-consciousness, then, is also other-consciousness. And if we recognize what is true, that the other is, in the first instance, an other self, we have escaped Descartes: we may say, indeed have to say *cogito te, ergo sumus.*

This additional recognition was not reached at once. It was the outcome of my student thinking and the theme of my first book. The formula just stated is incomplete, for it omits the ever present *aliquid,* the variable stuff, the sense-data perhaps, without which I know neither the "I" nor the "Thou": it might read *cogito aliquid in te,* or *cogito te per aliquid.* But the essential point is, if there is no "Thou" there is no "I"; and the effort of Descartes to prove the existence of God, having given that of the self, is mistaken and unnecessary.

This recognition appeared in various contexts during the early years of the century, as in Royce's striking use of Peirce's theory of Interpretation (in *The Problem of Christianity*). Later came Martin Buber's *Ich und Du.* Then the surprising insistence of Sartre and others that self-consciousness and other-consciousness are inseparable. So far as I know, these several bursts-through from Descartes' atomic individual—who, through Hugo Grotius and John Locke, has ruled much of the social and political thinking of modern times—were independent of each other, flickers of discovery only partially worked through. The Existentialist explosion directed itself mainly against another Cartesianism, the deterministic "science of man": man, say the Existentialists, is not a scientific object; he is made what he is by no causes, no heredity, no Nature, no Society, no God. He makes himself: his existence precedes every essence he accepts or invents. This suggests a defiant individualism— and it is defiant! But the inseparableness of the "I" and the "Thou" constitutes for Sartre the *angoisse,* the burden of responsibility for universalizing every such act of self-creation, which makes his ethical talk at times so reminiscent of Kant.

Professor Hartshorne plants this I-and-Thou principle in the middle of his metaphysics and at the same time of his ethics. But, as with Whitehead, it is for him a far more pervasive principle than in those other forms. It is not simply that the content of experience, the *aliquid,* inheres in another self, so that nature as a whole, with all its parts, constitutes a common object *between* the "I" and the total "Thou" of the world. It is that the very content of experience, the *aliquid* itself, is in its reality other-self, in innumerable examples: not merely is the world the living garment of God, but it is a vast congeries of *socii,* in which nothing is mere environment, or mere mechanical process, but every event and occasion is at its heart a living self. Everywhere is a sociality of selfhood which leaves personal identity and separate freedom intact.

Here is a key which promises to unlock many a door, whether in theology or in the general world-view, or in the dilemmas of a distracted world-mélange aspiring to become a world order. For this end, such clear, resolute and undespairing thinking as Hartshorne's is a necessary condition, and cannot but be a profound furtherance.

WILLIAM ERNEST HOCKING

Madison, N. H., August, 1950.

PREFACE

Although there has been a lapse of fifteen years between the writing of the earliest and the latest of these essays, they all seem rather shockingly consistent one with another. A man ought to learn some of the errors of his ways between the years thirty-seven and fifty-two of his existence. Or at least, he ought to shift some of his obsessions. But in this instance, it seems that much the same ideas recur with the difference of considerable advances (as I hope) in sharpness of definition and cogency of argument.

The main thesis, that reality is social process, is set forth in the first chapter. From the standpoint of method, a main import of all the essays is that we need to practice what might be called three-cornered thinking. Nearly all the questions that are important for our time are begged or confused by such crude or equivocal alternatives as—fascism versus communism (or even, capitalism versus socialism), naturalism versus supernaturalism, idealism versus realism. If we have made basic advances in intellectual method, and I think we have, in the last century or so, this should affect not merely our answers but our questions, to such an extent that the old dichotomies should be viewed with suspicion. The content of "nature," for instance, is not so obvious that the meaning of a contrasting term, "supernature," poses only the problem of acceptance or rejection. Again, that many meanings of "God" are intellectually untenable does not prove that all conceptions of a supreme reality worthy of worship must be so. It is limiting to look backward to the old fights with the hope of discerning the truth as a pure monopoly of one contender or the other. It is safer to employ what has been well termed the "double rejection," by which we are set free to look forward to the new alternatives that our resources, the accumulation of the ages, open to us. It should be our daring aspiration to rise above both sides of the old sterile disputes. What Feuerbach or Hume were fighting, we too may well find unacceptable, but such men failed to establish any logically coercive issue of the form: "agree with me or with my opponents." There are ideas scarcely dreamt of by either party. And if for Feuerbach and Hume we substitute Kant, Dewey, Russell, Morris Cohen, or Carnap, the principle still holds: there are religious doctrines that these men have neither accepted nor rejected consciously, because they have not been clearly aware of them. Philosophical issues cannot ultimately, I maintain, go thus by default. Sooner or later men will want to know what it is they accept, and what, in doing so, they reject, and why. It is my belief that our age has the privilege of producing a neglected alternative both to the old speculative theology or metaphysics, and to the mere rejection of all metaphysics and theology, an alternative as significantly new as relativity physics or quantum mechanics, yet attractive not simply in that it is new, but because it renders substantial justice to both parties in many an old battle. In other words, there is a novel "higher synthesis" which offers promise of being not merely one more doctrine to fight over, but, to some extent at least, a transcending of the causes of conflict. Many men have been creating this synthesis, and most of all, the late A. N. Whitehead. My own lesser degree of inventiveness is for others to assess, if they care to.

It may interest the reader, and also express my obligations to those from whom I have learned, if I indicate some of the steps by which I came to the type of philosophy embodied in this volume. Two of the basic ideas—that God is temporal as well as eternal, and that all reality is "psychic," or composed of some sort of feeling, volition, and the like—did not come to me originally from Whitehead. For the first idea, concerning God, I am indebted to my teacher, Professor Hocking, whose defense of the eternal-temporal view I found convincing; the second, and in a vague way the first idea as well, were beliefs arrived at largely prior to my acquaintance with academic philosophy, on the basis of reasoning from experience—stimulated, as it happened, by H. G. Wells, who at that time was passing through his temporary theistic phase. It seemed to me (then serving as orderly in an army hospital) that the facts of sympathy and of common aims (admitting the antipathies and conflicts then dramatized by the first World War) between men, and to some extent between sentient beings generally, were best explained by the notion that all wills somehow express and tend to fulfill one Will, all lives one Life. For a time, I thought that inorganic nature must (as Wells insisted) be something external to this supreme life or will; but I soon felt compelled to renounce such a dualism, for the single, and to me still conclusive, reason—which some philosophers, in particular Croce and Whitehead, have stressed, but which I did not consciously derive from any philosopher—that one may directly observe an esthetic unity of feeling between the self, and nature as immediately given, a unity which controverts the theory of a mind-matter duality. (Wordsworth's poetry—in a measure all poetry—seeks to express this insight). Now if the physical as given is essentially feeling, then, since thought can only expand, generalize, extrapolate, and abstract, it follows that thought can arrive at no world other than a world of feelings, with their relations, aspects, varieties, and so forth. This is, in one aspect, the social view of reality.

In Royce, I found versions of both the foregoing doctrines. But Royce assumed that for the inclusive or divine life even "future" events, or simply all events, are eternally real, and thus (as it seems to me would follow) not ultimately events, or becomings, but rather constituents of timeless being. W. E. Hocking, William James, and R. B. Perry cured me of any tendency to follow Royce on this point—and I think Dewey also would have been convincing here. Study with Husserl and Heidegger re-enforced my belief in the ultimate reality of temporal process. And as to the other conviction, that there is no absolute duality of mind and matter (since both as observed are composed of feeling), I noted that the neo-Kantian school (in Rickert) and Husserl's phenomenology (in his most famous disciple, Heidegger) had come to see, what Kant and Husserl themselves overlooked, that experience on the first level, which is prior to thought, is feeling in confrontation with feeling, feeling with a social structure, not cognition of bare facts or mere matter (whatever that would be) or mere neutral qualities or forms.

Then came the study of Peirce and Whitehead, begun at the same time and continued ever since. I found Peirce apparently undecided, and certainly unclear, as to the relation of God to time and becoming; but that reality is given and hence can only be thought (other than verbally) as "feelings" (in "reaction" with other feelings and functioning in "representations" or meanings) was emphatically Peirce's doctrine, so that once more this belief was confirmed. In Whitehead's *Process and Reality*, the temporal-eternal nature of deity at last received classic expression, in a philosophy developed in the grand manner. (Only later did I realize that Schelling, in *Ages of the World*, had come a good way in this direction; while at no time did Hegel's attempt to fuse eternity and time, the infinite and the finite, seem to me more than a vague or highly ambiguous indication of what needs to be done. Here the critcisms of C. I. Lewis—in a course on German Idealism—helped to put me on guard.) Peirce and Whitehead, it was pleasant to learn, both taught that the structure of reality is social through and through; but Whitehead had the fuller, sharper conception of this structure, in relation to facts of direct experience and scientific inference. And Whitehead had, what no other man had ever had, as it seems: a complete, all-sided, explicit conception of social *process* as the concrete ultimate mode of reality, of which mere "being" is always an abstract element, or, in the less abstract cases, a deposit or fixed resultant. Of course, Bergson had this idea also, and others; but they were not able to do justice to the elements of being, stability, and identity, which, though nothing apart from process, are by no means nothing or negligible *in* process. (On the other hand, it may be that in his theory of "eternal objects," Whitehead slightly compromises the "principle of process" which he shares with Bergson. In Peirce's theory that definite abstract forms evolve from a primordial continuum of indefinite potentiality, I have hoped one could see a corrective of Whitehead on this point.)

The pragmatism of Peirce, James, and Dewey has scarcely had a crucial effect upon the writing of these essays (I incline to think that what is valid in pragmatism is largely contained in Whitehead), but at least it has reinforced the antipathy to verbal exaltations of "eternity," "being," "absoluteness," or "perfection," unrelated to meanings relevant to living—to volition, aspiration, and love. All of these thinkers, with Whitehead, agree at many points, such as: the partial indeterminacy in process, the relevance of all genuine meanings to action, and the supreme value of what Dewey calls "shared experience"— only that he does not see that this last is a cosmological as well as an ethical principle, or that in some lowly form it is present even in "inorganic" nature. The social view means that sympathy is a universal phenomenon, though it is sometimes very rudimentary, and sometimes qualified strongly by antipathy.

To one philosophic influence nearly all of us have been exposed, especially if, as in my case, we have studied and taught in Europe. Yet there are some things which a student of the philosophers mentioned can not have needed to learn from "Existentialism." Surely not that man is indeterminate and self-caused (Sartre); for all the philosophers named above have insisted upon this. Dewey going perhaps as far as Sartre in regard to human beings, and Whitehead holding the metaphysical doctrine that every creature is in some degree self-created and a new reality every moment. Indeed, for Whitehead, each experience is a numerically different actuality from its predecessors. Also James, at least, had much of the suspicion of "system" that is found in so-called Existentialists. True, none of the Americans or English had said that the "nothing nullifies," *das Nichts nichtet*, and I do not wish to say that this adds "nothing" to our wisdom! There may indeed be some value in the unparalleled frankness with which certain writers insist upon the absolute irrationality of life, headed for death, on the assumption that there is no sort of everlasting life to constitute the permanent resultant of our having lived. But James, Peirce, and Whitehead had pointed out, in their several ways, very incisively that the only conceivable rational meaning is in connection with some everlasting community of life, apart from which our action is only a "passing whiff of insignificance" (Whitehead). Dewey alone has refused to face this issue, save in the vaguest language, and then but rarely.

The priority of "existence" over "essence," from which the
name Existentialism derives, is affirmed by all four thinkers
just mentioned. However, the English language has an advantage here (alas not usually exploited by philosophers) over
at least the French. In common speech we tend to use "existence" somewhat differently from "actuality" (German *Wirk-
lichkeit*), in a fashion which suggests that the strict alternative
to essence or possibility is not existence but actuality. (To be
safe from ambiguity, one must say "Actualism," not "Existentialism.") It is indeed true that what is actual cannot be inferred from a logical possibility or fixed nature; actuality is
always an accident, logically speaking, a brute fact. But the
word "accident" suggests an event, a happening; and we do not
say normally that events "exist," rather we say they occur or
are actual. They are Whitehead's "actual entities." In Chapter
Fourteen it is shown that this distinction between actuality and
existence is not trivial, but is essential to any clarity in metaphysics. For instance, it enables us to reconcile the "necessity"
of God's existence with the contingency of all, even divine, actuality. This is an example of the way old issues are transcended
by the new insights now available. It is notable that when Sartre
says, through one of his characters, that God, if he existed,
would be "in a situation with respect to man," that is, would
be relative to man and dependent for some of his actual qualities upon the accidents of man's history, the French author is
affirming something that numerous modern philosophers and
theologians, for example, Whitehead and Berdyaev, emphatically accept and insist upon. (Even "neo-orthodoxy," in speaking of an "encounter" with God, may be implying the same
thing.) Sartre is here expressing a profound theological insight, which suggests that his atheism is primarily a protest
against the old absolutistic theology, with its supposition that
God in his actuality or total reality is simply independent of
and unrelated to man.

It has been encouraging to discover in recent years that not
only Schelling, but also (among others): Fechner and the
German theologian, Pfleiderer; in France Jules Lequier and
Renouvier; and many writers in England and the United States,
have had ideas of God more or less similar to that which I de-

fend. Thus it seems that a new "natural theology" is growing up, which is about equally distinct from the old naturalism and the old supernaturalism. It is perhaps as far from Barth's new version of revealed theology as from the kinds of natural theology which he rejects (the only kind, at any rate, he shows much awareness of). It is considerably closer to the (miscalled?) "neo-orthodoxy" of Tillich and Niebuhr, and not very far from what appear—on the basis of a recent lecture and two brief conversations—to be the present views of Nygren, though if I am not misled in this, it follows that his famous *Eros and Agape* is in some respects an unfortunate embodiment of his doctrine.

To Berdyaev I am close, except for his reliance upon "mythical" language, and his failure to see that the old rationalism misconceived the God of religion, the God of love and responsiveness and interaction with men—not because, as Berdyaev inclines to think, this rationalism was too insistent upon logical criteria, and too fearful of paradoxes, or apparent contradictions, but for the opposite reason, because its logic was bad, and because it was too tolerant of contradictions. The really insuperable paradoxes, we begin to see, are in the idea of "The Absolute," not in that of "God." The common saying, "the God of philosophy is a quite different thing from the God of religion," is now antiquated, or at least, must be given a partly new meaning; since philosophy, in a long list of its modern and especially recent representatives, has for reasons of its own criteria of intelligibility made the great transition from a conception of God as devoid of relativity and *becoming* to the conception of Him as in his full actuality the supreme relativity and *becoming*, the supreme subject of social relationships and interactions—though not, for all that, without an aspect of eternity, necessity, absoluteness and independence.

Is the philosophy of this book Christian? Perhaps the question should be left to the experts on the meaning of that term? Like other words, it can be and is defined variously. I do believe that the new religious philosophy is rather more in the spirit of the Gospels than was the older type of Supernaturalist Theology, which with many scholars I hold to be an inconsistent compound of Greek-philosophical postulates and bibli-

cal religious insights. The new tradition in philosophy eliminates the postulates that created this inconsistency, for it finds
them inconsistent in themselves, quite apart from religious
values and beliefs. Hence the problem of Christianity is in
some degree a fresh problem for philosophy. However, I have
no Christology to offer, beyond the simple suggestion that Jesus
appears to be the supreme symbol furnished to us by history of
the notion of a God genuinely and literally "sympathetic" (incomparably *more* literally than any man ever is), receiving
into his own experience the sufferings as well as the joys of the
world. It might also be well to say that, while I cannot accept
Trinitarianism as it stands, I do not think that what was wrong
with it is rectified merely by going back to the old way of conceiving God as bare Unity. Rather, in so far as the three Persons implied an inner social life of deity, a believer in the
social theory of reality must think there was truth in the idea.
(See Chapters Eight and Ten.) But he must also hold (with
Berdyaev) that the notion of this divine life as having nothing
temporal about it, or as involving no social relativity of God
to the world as well as of God to God, tended to spoil the doctrine.

Thus, once more, the old controversies may be now mostly
sterile; we have fresh issues, and therefore a chance to find
fresh truths. It is not enough now to go back to one's great
grandfather, whoever he may be. The old metaphysicians and
dogmatists sought, or claimed to have found, eternal truths,
but in this search or claim they seem to have made numerous,
and one hopes far from eternal, mistakes! On the other hand,
it is interesting that theologians of repute, including at least
one noted for his conservative inclinations, have told me that
they see no necessary incompatibility between the new religious philosophy and the Christian faith, although they admit
that the reading of Augustine, Aquinas, Calvin, Kant, or Schlei-
ermacher would scarcely disclose this philosophy. Perhaps our
forefathers were neither so right as the orthodox, nor so wrong
as their opponents, usually suppose.

If it be asked what technical "ism" the book professes, I
should have to reply that, since the old alternatives are repu-
diated, only some new term could serve, such as "societism"

for the theory that reality is essentially social, or "superrealism" or "surrelativism" for the theory that deity, or the categorically supreme individual, is neither absolute nor relative in the old sense, but a synthesis of absolute and relative. Not "absolutism," but "relativism," in a new sense, is the last word; precisely because, in this new sense, it can include all the absolutism there seems need to admit or possibility consistently to conceive.

Several of the essays have been more or less extensively altered, sometimes including the title, from their previously published form. Except for the first two paragraphs, the essay on Whitehead is new. In the rest there are some omissions, partly to reduce duplication of content, and some additions, chiefly to provide continuity from one essay to another. I have ventured accordingly to speak of "chapters," rather than merely of essays. The arrangement is not chronological, but so far as possible systematic. There is some order and progression of argument through the book. Thus the position is outlined in Chapter One, approached from the standpoint of esthetic phenomena in Chapter Two, and from that of social psychology and biology in Chapter Three. Chapter Four explains and defends the sense in which the doctrine combines "realism" and "idealism." Chapter Five sets forth the factor of chance (contingency, indeterminacy) posited by the theory, shows how chance inevitably results in an element of tragedy in process in spite of any providence there may be, and how providence must be conceived in this connection; further, how love (as religion told us long ago and psychoanalysis is telling us now) is the supreme motivation, and how it unites with chance, incompatibility, and the resulting mixture of tragedy and joy, to form a realistic design for living. Chapter Six, and in simpler fashion Chapter Nine, present the Superrelativist or *Panentheist* conception of the absolute and relative aspects of deity. Chapter Seven sums up the social view of reality once more, with special emphasis upon religious implications. Readers primarily concerned with religion, and untrained in philosophical technicalities, might perhaps begin with this chapter, continuing to the end of the book, before reading the chapters in Part One. Chapter Eight applies the doctrine to the question

of "Christianity," with some slight reference to the Ecumenical
Movement of *rapprochement* among the churches. Chapter Ten
deals with the relations of Reason, Faith, and Revelation (also
discussed in Chapter Seven), and the next three chapters under-
take a brief critique of "humanism" in religion, with Dewey
and Russell as case studies. Chapter Fourteen explains why
Whitehead's idea of deity and of immortality is religiously
"available" in spite of all that has been said to the contrary.

The principal gap in the argument of the book is that only
suggestions or brief outlines of "proofs for the existence of God"
will be found within its covers. (See, for example, Chapter
Thirteen.) This is because I wish to devote a volume to this
topic alone. What is done in the following pages is to show that
only one sort of idea of God *could* possibly denote a reality,
and to show how this idea can form the central factor in a general view of existence which seems intelligible and able to
inspire living, and which illuminates some of the basic features
of life and nature as revealed by modern knowledge.

—CHARLES HARTSHORNE

Part I: PHILOSOPHICAL PRINCIPLES

CHAPTER ONE

THE SOCIAL
CONCEPTION OF THE UNIVERSE

W HO HAS NOT heard of the scientific conceptions of our time, such as evolution, relativity, the quantum? Less widely known but perhaps even more important, are some ideas that are due not so much to modern science as to modern philosophy. These philosophical ideas have been less widely publicized than the scientific, partly because philosophers disagree, so that their views carry less authority than those of natural scientists. Yet even in science disagreements occur, and even in philosophy disagreement is not absolute. Moreover, as men do not cease to take food although good drinking-water is easier to obtain, so they should not ignore philosophy merely because agreement is easier to reach in science. Philosophy and science, like food and water, have different functions. And since every man (or at any rate, every thoughtful man) must have a working philosophy of life, why should he not have the benefit of knowing something of what professionals in the subject are doing?

The scientist asks, what ideas will fit and explain the facts? The philosopher asks, what ideas will explain the ideas that fit the facts, and in addition, will explain the ideas which do not fit the facts? The philosopher is seeking principles so general, so basic, that they are no longer special cases to be explained by more general principles, but are themselves the most general of ideas, true not only of the actual world but of any conceivable one. Since there is nothing beyond them, nothing more fundamental, those ideas must, taken together, be self-explanatory.

They form a system which sets forth the ultimate what? how? and why? (in whatever sense there can be such ultimates.) Because this system (if only we can find it) is completely general, it can deal with values as well as facts, with God as well as man, with the everlasting as well as the temporary, with the possible as well as the actual.

The philosophical system would not be a completed version of science, for it can contain only general principles, not specific facts.[1] Thus philosophy does not compete with science. Nor can science take the place of philosophy, as can be seen from this alone, that scientific knowledge by itself gives no satisfaction to the man who reflects intelligently upon death. Since all paths lead to the same end, the grave, what does it really matter how we live? True, we may help those who come after us, but they too will die, and, according to astronomers, even the race can hardly survive forever on this planet. What then is the relation of temporary values to the ultimate "long run" of things? To answer this question rationally we must know the very nature of time and of the other basic aspects of existence. We must have a philosophy.

Science explains facts by such ideas as "matter," "law," and "experience" or "observation." But are these ideas, as used by scientists, fully generalized, or are they special cases? Is *all* reality matter in motion, or can there be "immaterial" spirits? Can there be lawless matter or experience; what are the most general relations between matter, experience, and law? These are some of the questions that a scientist would hardly wish to consider, but which philosophy takes as its own. It seeks a set of ideas of which *any* scientific or common-sense notions, true or false, can be viewed as special cases. For example, materialism is the philosophy which regards "matter in motion" as the general principle, and experience, mind, purpose, as special cases. Idealism, on the other hand, makes mind the general principle, and matter the special case. Similarly, the philosophical doctrine of determinism views law or causal order as completely universal, and treats freedom as the special case where the laws happen to

---

1. Even God, so far as dealt with in pure philosophy, is not a special fact but a general principle. See my book, *The Divine Relativity*, pp. 30-34, 79-82.

govern motives and acts of will; whereas libertarianism makes freedom the rule, and treats law as the special case where freedom is slight, resulting in approximate or statistical uniformities. It is possible to combine the positive elements of the various philosophical positions. Perhaps all reality is both physical and psychical, and perhaps everywhere there is both law and freedom. In that case, the extremes of doctrine might cease to exist as extremes. Thus, in physics the strife between wave and particle theories of light has been resolved by a "both . . . and."

It is a similar merging of apparently contrary doctrines in a "higher synthesis" that I believe is happening in philosophy. I do not say that all, or even a majority, of philosophers would today accept the doctrine I am about to explain. What I say is that no other equally definite and comprehensive view of the universe has resulted from modern philosophizing. Some of its creators or spokesmen are Charles Peirce, James Ward, W. P. Montague; Whitehead is its Einstein, Leibniz was its Newton; other great forerunners were Schelling (in his later period, beginning in 1811), Fechner, William James, and Bergson. Ideas related to it are found in leading contemporary theologians, such as Berdyaev and Niebuhr, and also in some leading natural scientists.

There is a conception in which motion and mind, law and freedom, are inextricably blended. It is the conception of the "social," or rather it is what this conception becomes when fully generalized. First, let us note that every society has its routine, its laws or customary ways of behaving. Without such routine, such enduring and common ways of acting, there would not be cooperation or mutual understanding, but only mutual frustration or absolute indifference, in other words, no society. But the routine of a society is never absolute; it permits creative departure from the norm or the usual. Individual caprice is kept within bounds, but it is not eliminated. The higher the society, the more notable in it are the unique individuals who break through the merely customary and predictable with the novel and hitherto unimagined. (Consider Beethoven composing the *Fifth Symphony*.) Here we have an idea that can explain any conceivable degree of relative orderliness or of freedom. In a society with members on a very low level of existence, their individual freedom will be correspondingly slight, and the element of law will predominate to such an extent that to an observer with imperfect means of observation (almost any observer except God) there may appear to be no freedom whatever. Given, at the other extreme, a society of superior individuals, say of geniuses, obviously the element of customary, predictable routine will there be at a minimum. But not absent altogether! For if it were, the society must cease to function as such, as it also must cease to function if routine became so absolute as to destroy individuality, and all interest in living, through intolerable monotony. Thus the social idea covers all possibilities except the unthinkable extreme of zero order, or pure chaos, and the opposite extreme of zero freedom, or absolute determinism. Whether or not absolute determinism is thinkable (and there are reasons for doubting that it is), at least we can say that it could never be verified. All observation falls short of absolute precision and hence no observation can detect the absolute validity of any law. Accordingly, the social idea covers all the relations of law and freedom which might conceivably be observed. Any society with very low-grade members will to many observers appear to lack freedom, and will lend itself to highly definite predictions. It will thus appear to be not a society but a "merely mechanical" system. What then is to show that this is not the case with the human observer confronting whatever is humanly regarded as dead matter or mere mechanism? However— some will object— this at most only shows that the social philosophy *may* be true, not that it is true. But consider: the situation is that nothing could conceivably be known by any observer not to be social; whereas the social character of some things, such as human groups, can be and is known. (Some will deny that we can know human freedom to be real, but the social philosophy has cogent means of dealing with this objection. And at least we can know that human beings are social in the sense of having sympathetic feelings, and, as we shall see, it cannot be known that any part of nature is without such feelings.)

Thus our contention is that the social category fits all actual or conceivable facts of observation, while non-social conceptions are at best required by no conceivable observations and contradicted by some. Critics of the social philosophy who complain that we cannot detect definite social character in all portions of nature are missing the main point, which is that an idea actually known to be true in some cases, but not even potentially known to be false in any *conceivable* case, is for all purposes an ultimate idea. Obviously, limited minds such as ours could not verify in detail all applications of an ultimate concept. To demand this is to demand the impossible and the unnecessary. It is to misunderstand the philosophical problem.

But perhaps you say: "God, at least, might know some things to be strictly mechanical or non-social." The social philosophy replies: "We must first determine what sort of God is really conceivable, and what, in accordance with this conceivable nature, he might conceivably know." And the social philosophy has arguments to show that the only conceivable God is a social being whose creatures must also be social throughout. We shall have something to say about this theological question later. Meanwhile, you may further object that even to us human beings it is plain that a stone or a body of water is not a social being or a society. But are you quite sure? As has been shown above, low-grade societies must appear as non-social to any observer whose manner of observing is too inaccurate to detect their minute elements of freedom. With sufficiently improved techniques of observations and inference, however, the absence of any complete routine (which is the negative side of freedom) will begin to appear. Now this seems to have happened in twentieth-century physics. The uncertainty principle and the impossibility of conceiving (not merely, as some say, of verifying) any but statistical uniformities in microphysics are now commonplace, and (as has been widely admitted by physicists themselves) they break down the assumption of a difference in principle between social and mechanical laws. Thus, a social scientist, writing not in defense of the social philosophy but with another objective, is able to say: "The social sciences do not need to be brought to the level of the natural sciences; they are already there as far as the logical structure of their laws is concerned. . . . This level is not the mythological level of absolute certainty and predictability but that of statistical averages and probability. . . . The new physics show, indeed, that there exists a close correspondence between the human mind, on the one hand, and nature and society on the other. Modern scientific thought re-establishes the unity of the physical and social world."[2] Is the reader still so certain that a stone is not an example of the social?

However, it may seem that the logical structure of the laws involved should not be made the only test of sociality. So it will be well to consider the matter more broadly. Let us define the social as the appeal of life for life, of experience for experience. It is "shared experience," the echo of one experience in another. Hence nothing can be social that is without experience. The minimum of experience, let us further agree, is feeling. Creatures are social if they feel, and feel in relation to each others' feelings. Can this be true, as the social philosophy holds, of *all* things?

We can hardly doubt that the higher animals, at least, have feelings. And there is evidence that they have some sympathetic sharing in the feelings of others, for experts tell us that social behavior can be followed far down the animal scale, perhaps to the very bottom. But is not a nervous system necessary to feeling? Can animals lacking such a system feel pleasure or pain? It is safe to say that animals so different from us as not to have a brain must, if they have an inner life of feeling at all, have very different feelings from ours. For physiology is the clue to psychology. Yet, if a very different physiological make-up proves a very different psychological make-up, it does not prove the absence of any psychological nature at all. Animals with no stomach nevertheless digest food, animals with no lungs can use oxygen. So we see (what is evident in itself) that lack of a specialized organ need not mean absence of the function which the organ when present fulfills; it may only mean that the function is performed in a less specialized way, on a simpler, more elementary level. A nervous system is a specialized organ of feeling and volition; as muscles are specialized organs of movement. But as animals without muscles can nevertheless move, so those without nerves may feel, and may move in accordance with those feelings. So long as

---

2. Hans J. Morgenthau, *Ethics*, April, 1944.

there is response to stimuli, what is to prove that the response lacks feeling? There are animals which have no nerves of touch, yet they act as though they felt what touched them. A single-celled animal moves as a whole, though it has neither nerves nor muscles; it takes account of its environment, though it has no brain. What can tell us (or any observer) that it does not have feeling, for instance of pleasantness and unpleasantness, in the presence of various stimuli? Of course, the farther from ourselves is any animal, the less definite must be our conception of its psychological nature. Comparative psychology cannot perhaps derive much profit from considering the joys and sorrows of an amoeba. But this is hardly evidence that the amoeba neither suffers nor enjoys. It is rather evidence that the human mind is not as the divine "to whom all hearts are open," and all feelings equally comprehensible.

There are, it is true, certain many-celled animals without brains—such as some of the lower worms—which seem not in any pronounced fashion to act as wholes, and often not to feel what is happening to their various parts. But this may only mean that while the various cells, which do act as wholes, may for all we know, have feelings, there is probably no feeling which is felt by the whole animal. A similar interpretation is applicable to the many-celled plants. Each of the cells of a tree has more functional unity than the whole tree. As Whitehead puts it, "a tree is a democracy." An animal, at least a vertebrate animal, is not a democracy; for its cells are strongly subordinated to the whole animal acting as a unit—its feelings, desires, perhaps thoughts and purposes. A man's mind is king over his cells. Plants, and some low animals, may have no such masterminds ruling over their cells. Yet each cell has functional unity, and may have its own master-mind ruling over the molecules composing it. On this view, a plant does not "bend towards the light"; its cells bend because those on the sunny side respond to the stimulus of light. What takes place is a group reaction, so far as we can determine. Thus, a creature may be a society of cells, and so conform to the social philosophy even though it is not itself a member of any society.

The same formula applies to the so-called "inorganic" parts of nature. A stone cannot plausibly be regarded as member of any society. But it may *be* a society. It is naive to suppose that, merely because molecules, atoms, etc., are invisibly small, they cannot be social beings, in relation to their neighbors, or their constituents, or both. But, you may object, molecules are not even alive in the physical sense, and so they can hardly have any psychic or social life. How, then, do we define "life"? Response to environment, adaptation, seeking and avoiding reactions, these perhaps may be included in our definition. But certainly atoms and even elementary particles in some sense respond to their environments; certainly they avoid some things and move towards others. Physicists speak of the "satisfied state" of an atom. It cannot be science which shows us that no sort of satisfaction in the psychological sense is there.

But what, you may wonder, is the social account of that bodily aspect of things which we call "matter"—that something which is spread out in space, which has shape and size and motion, in contrast to mind, which (it appears) has no size or shape, and cannot move or be located in space? This, however, has been pronounced a false dualism by many masters of scientific and philosophical reasoning. Some fragments only of the argument may be mentioned here. To science "a thing is where it immediately acts," and our minds do act immediately, by all the evidence, and at definite places—upon parts of our bodies. Hence the mind has place, and indeed is in many places at once; and from this, shape, size, and motion follow, for the shape and size of a thing are determined by the pattern of places which it occupies at a given moment, and its motion by the places which it occupies in successive moments. It can be inferred with some probability that the human mind, at any given moment, is not drastically different in size and shape from the pattern of activity in the nervous system with which at that moment it interacts, and as this activity moves about somewhat it follows that the mind literally moves in brain and nerves, though in ways unimaginably various and intricate. On the other hand, "inanimate" matter consists of electrons and other particles, and the question, what is the size and shape of an electron? is if anything even more difficult to answer than the similar question about the human mind. True, an electron is more sharply located in space, but this is easily explicable on the assumption that the electron, too, is a social being endowed with sentience. For the lowest-grade social beings will be those which have none below them over which they rule, and thus they will have no "body" formed by a society of subordinates over which their direct action will extend and in this manner acquire extension in space. The electron is thus a sort of point of energy or, as it were, a disembodied spirit, and though physicists speak of its "radius" this seems merely to indicate a critical boundary in its mode of interaction with other particles. Thus, neither the denial of spatial properties to high-grade social entities, nor the ascription of literal spatiality to the lowest types of entity, such as matter consists of, are free of serious difficulties from the standpoint of present-day knowledge.

Of course, it might be objected that the human mind has spatial character only thanks to its association with the body, and hence through matter, which thus appears as the primary subject of spatial characters. But the argument can be turned the other way around. My mind is where my body is, but where is my body? My body is that portion of nature with which "I" have most immediate and intimate transactions. I do not start with my body and thence go on to find my mind. I start with some feeling or sensing of myself as desiring, purposing, suffering, enjoying, and doing these things in association with phenomena which disclose what I call my body. Extension is primitively given, not in mere matter, but in enjoyed, suffered matter, matter connected with mind, and all spatial location works from the "here" which is determined by my personality, or interest, or focus of attention, to a "there" separated from the direct action of this personality by a greater or less interval. All matter is in a definite place for me so far as I can connect it with "my" body not just as body, but as mine, as the one which is within the scope of my intimate transactions. So it is false to say that mind has locus only because matter has. Rather "locus," for matter, has only so much meaning as interaction with minds can give it. It is not in mere dead matter but in living experience that "spread-outness" is initially observed. On the whole, then, there seems to be no genuine scientific or rational support for the doctrine that something besides societies of minds is required to explain the "extension" and motion attributed to matter. The nervous system is not indeed our human mind, but it may, for all any conceivable science could show, be a society of sub-human minds over which the human mind rules as in some degree their master.

We have mentioned that some societies are democracies, that is, lacking in any ruling member, whereas others, for example, the society of cells forming the human body, possess such a member. We may call the non-democratic societies "monarchies." In one sense, the word is far too weak, since no human monarch has ever had anything like the power over his kingdom which the human personality, for example, has over its bodily cells. On the other hand, the literal meaning of "sole ruler" must not be taken to mean that the ruled are powerless, have no control over themselves or each other. What is meant is that their power is radically subordinate to the one power whose effective field of operations is the society as a whole. They are imperfect and local powers in contrast to the superior quality and universal sway of the ruling power. As a result of this subordination to a superior, in a monarchical society the entire group acts with a functional unity comparable or superior to that of the various members. From this we see the important principle that unusual unity of action can be imposed upon a society by a dominant member. But we see something else, if we consider closely. This is that a portion or sub-class of a monarchical society may in itself be a democracy. Thus, the cells of the heart, though they act together, do so only in crude fashion as compared to the unity of action found in the growth and self-maintenance of the single cells composing the heart. No ruling member of the heart society, it seems, imposes unity of action upon the society, though the ruler of the entire body, the human personality, does of course, influence the heart action. Now this suggests the idea that all societies, however democratic, may be portions of an all-inclusive monarchical society, the entire universe, with order imposed throughout by a single dominant all-ruling member.

It is indeed difficult if not impossible to see how a democratic society can exist except within a larger monarchical one. (Lest prejudices be awakened at this point, it should be explained that this is not an argument for political monarchy but rather an argument against it; for the existence of a super-human monarch makes a human one unnecessary, as the ancient Jews were told by one of their prophets. Nor is "theocracy" in the usual sense of government by priests a consequence of our doctrine. God's sway over all beings is direct, as well as through priestly or other intermediaries, and the role of the latter is a question to be settled solely on its merits—or demerits.) The members of a democracy which is merely that, in other words, which lacks an imposed ruler, would not be compelled to cooperate. Would they even be able to do so? Nothing would guarantee the continuance of the society from moment to moment save the infinite good luck that they all happened to use their freedom in ways serviceable to the society. Each would have to be quite uncertain that its own efforts to serve the society would not be indefinitely nullified by the direction taken by the actions of others. If there were in the universe no radically dominant member, able to set limits to the chaotic possibilities of individual freedom, it seems there would be no reason why the scheme of things should not dissolve in a chaos of unmitigated conflict, that is to say, in the cessation of all feeling and activity through the irresistible force of unbearable frustration. And the farther the descent toward confusion, the more helpless would the members become to remedy the situation—the less, for example, could each be aware of the direction likely to be taken by the others (for perception and knowledge depend upon order) and so the less could each know what was required to restore the order of the society. The trouble would therefore be the opposite of self-remedying. Hence it seems clear that the universe as a going concern must be a monarchical society, if it is a society at all. (And that it is *not* a society is, we have argued, a radically unverifiable, and hence, useless, supposition.)

What we have arrived at is the question of the existence and nature of God, as it arises in any philosophy based on the social conception of reality. Practically all who have held such a philosophy have thought that it requires the conception of God as the ultimate ruler of the world society. Democratic cooperation is possible only within an all-inclusive monarchy. As remarked above, this monarchy is cosmic, and has nothing to do with political monarchy. The "monarch" sees to it that there is enough involuntary or unconscious cooperation to make voluntary forms of cooperation possible without intolerable risks. Men can freely decide to aid each other in this way or in that because it is decided for them that, whatever they do, the basic cooperations that maintain the cosmic society will go on.

The conception of God which our argument leads to is that of a social being, dominant or ruling over the world society, yet not merely from outside, in a tyrannical or non-social way; but rather as that member of the society which exerts the supreme conserving and coordinating influence. This is not quite the traditional theological idea of God; though it is, I believe, the religious idea. For religion, as a concrete practical matter, as a way of life, has generally viewed God as having social relations with man, as sympathizing with him and gaining something through his achievements. God was interested in man, therefore could be "pleased" or "displeased," made more or less happy, by man's success or failure, and could thus be "served" by human efforts. Technical theology, however, for long ages contradicted this practical working idea of God by defining him in strictly non-social terms. He was said to be absolutely perfect independently of man, incapable of receiving from man any good or evil. It was then inconsistent to speak of divine love. For to love a being yet be absolutely independent of and unaffected by its welfare or suffering seems nonsense. Indeed, the very act of creation by such a God must be absurd and meaningless. A being which contains, in sheer independence of others, all possible perfection and value must surely know better than to clutter up existence with beings which can add nothing to the value that would exist without them. Such absurdities, and many others, have almost destroyed the intellectual prestige of the older types of theology.

The socially oriented philosophy of our period puts the whole matter upon a new level, free from the difficulties referred to. God is not viewed as a being that could exist in solitary independence, but as the being uniquely able to maintain the society of which it is member, the *only* social being unconditionally able to guarantee the survival, the minimal integrity, of its society, and of itself as member of that society. This is a new definition of omnipotence. It means power adequate to preserve the society no matter what other members may do. It does not mean, power to prevent any and all evil or conflict; for social power, even in the perfect form, is still social, that is, it is power to set limits to the freedom of others, but not to destroy all freedom; and where there is freedom, however sharply limited, conflict and evil must always be possible. What God can do, and because he is good does do, is to set the best or optimal limits to freedom (as any good government will do, in its drastically more limited providence). The definition of "optimal limits" is that they are such that, were more freedom allowed, the risks would increase more than the opportunities, and were less freedom allowed, the opportunities would decrease more than the risks. If it be asked, must the risk in our human case include the possibility of race suicide? one can only reply, who knows? But some risk there must be if there is to be any opportunity, any existence in the social sense. Thus, the problem of evil (at least in its most acute form) appears as a false problem due to a faulty or non-social definition of omnipotence.

Another ancient problem illuminated by the social philosophy is that of death and immortality. It is often said that the consolation for death is children, and posterity in general, by whom one's influence is prolonged beyond death. But suppose the whole human race dies, and there is thus finally no posterity? Besides, posterity is but a poor receptacle for our values as we depart this life. What will most of our lives mean to those who come after us, who will know little of these lives and care less? The real death is indeed something which we undergo every minute, and for which there is no human remedy. This death is forgetting. The value of life is in the experiences of living; but these experiences perish almost as fast as they are born. At any moment I forget (or at least fail vividly to remember) all but a negligible portion of my past life. Thus, I possess but a tiny fraction of the value that has been mine. Is the rest lost; is what was once so much now so nearly nothing?

The only answer that meets the conditions of the question is the religious answer, properly understood. There was a saint

who was willing to be damned for the glory of God; and I de-
voutly believe that the only way rationally to accept death is to
see that though at every moment, through forgetting, we yield
up, die to, most of our previous reality; the forgotten experiences are not thereby lost, since they are one and all additions
to the experiences of God, the all-cherishing or cosmically social being, to whom all hearts—not only as they are but as they
have been—are open. (The older theology could not give this
answer; for it held that nothing we do or are can add to the
perfection of God, who would have been just as complete had
we never existed.)

On the view just outlined, the young lives which are tragically terminated in war before coming to normal human com-
pletion are nevertheless, so far as they have gone, not wasted,
and their value does not lie merely in the service their military
victory may render to posterity, great as that service can be.
The value does not even depend necessarily upon "immortality"
in the conventional sense. It depends rather upon this, that all
the beauty of their past experience, all the delights and shades
of feeling, none exactly duplicating those of any other child or
youth, are added once for all to the store-house of beauties
which is the divine memory, wherein all that we are is destined,
in spite of our faults, to be imperishably loved by the cosmically
social being, the one whose zest for the varieties of life is inexhaustible, and from whose consciousness nothing can die
away and be lost. (To be sure, suffering and evil are also retained, but the *total* quality of experience is never negative.
When existence offers *no* reward, consciousness lapses. God, as
we shall see, suffers, but joy predominates.) Posterity will be
important for the same reason that we are important, because
it and we have an ultimate posterity which is deathless, the
endless future life of God. Conventional immortality, whether
it be real or not, fails to meet the essential need, which is not
escape from bodily dissolution, but from loss of precious experiences. Only a socially constituted, all-retaining memory can
give all of life a long-run meaning, and only a socially constituted deity can have such a memory. That the divine memory,
unlike others, retains all, is inherent in its cosmic or supreme
status.

In view of the persistent and often violent disagreements among philosophers it would be presumptuous to offer the social view as proved. But it has sufficient following among those who have mastered modern knowledge to be intellectually respectable, and it has such intrinsic attractions that as it becomes better known it may well gain much wider acceptance. In a democracy, at least, men have a right to know something of what the experts are accomplishing—all the more when the results achieved, even though inconclusive and not agreed upon, are able to inspire and satisfy those seeking rational meaning for our human lives.

CHAPTER TWO

HARMONY IN LIFE AND NATURE

T HE TOPICS discussed in the previous chapter are
now to be viewed in terms of esthetic principles. Why in these
terms? One reason is as follows: If experience is the source of
meanings, then the basic traits of experience must somehow
correspond to the basic possible meanings, and these to the
basic structure of any world that can be meant. Now all experience is concerned with value. Experience is an act; and every
act at least strives to realize a value. What basically is value? It
cannot be ethical value that is basic; for ethics is concerned with
consequences or with justice to others; and the goodness or bad-
ness of these consequences, or the good and bad that is to be
justly distributed, must be measured by a criterion other than
the ethical. Moreover, infants and animals experience and enjoy value, but are not ethical beings. The study that concerns
itself with value in its universal character is esthetics, taken in
the broadest sense. Esthetic value is immediate value, and this
all experience must present, and to this all mediate value must
lead.[1]

One may also put the matter as does Croce. Esthetic experience is intuitive, concrete; esthetics is the science of the laws of
direct awareness or intuition as such. But all abstract knowledge presupposes intuitive awareness. Hence, esthetics etablishes
data that all abstract knowledge must take into account if its
basis in immediacy is to be understood. And unless this basis
is understood, we cannot know what the abstractness of the

---

1. An excellent recent discussion of this is given by C. I. Lewis in *An Analysis
of Knowledge and Valuation* (1946), Chaps. XIII-XV.

knowledge consists in, what it is of concrete reality that is omitted. Hence, as Whitehead, Vasconcellos, and some others (among the first, Schelling) have seen, esthetics is basic to metaphysics and cosmology.

A complete esthetics would have to consist of at least three partially distinct but closely interrelated theories: the theory of esthetic qualities (such as those of color or sound or smell), the theory of esthetic structures (such as those formed by combinations of colors or sounds or tastes), and the theory of esthetic meanings ("expression").

The theory of esthetic structures might be called the theory of harmony, for "harmony" is the description we give to the most successful esthetic combinations. In this essay the problem of harmony is to be made central, neglecting almost entirely the important phases of that problem which depend for their solution upon a developed theory of expression, and a theory of quality.

What is harmony? It would probably be agreed that it is a kind of relation between things such that though they are felt to be different from each other, they are yet felt to be not merely different. Otherness is not the only relation between them. In fact, it seems that the very opposite of otherness is also involved. In analogous color harmony, the basis of the harmony is clearly the fact that the different hues are all variations of one general color, such as the variations of green in foliage. Again, in poetic rhyme it is clearly the similarity as well as the difference between two sound groups that makes the esthetic effect. With musical chords it is also true that octaves, at least, seem similar as truly as they seem different. They may in fact actually be mistaken for each other! The trouble with this example is that octaves are rather insipid as harmonies, taken by themselves. Perhaps octaves are too similar? The more exciting thirds or fourths are also similar, but less so. This is a defensible view, as I have argued elsewhere.[2] But we have also the problem of complementary color harmony. Is there similarity between two complementary colors? It is clear that there is some, for at least both are colors. Fur-

---

2. In *The Philosophy and Psychology of Sensation*, §33.

thermore, both may be of equal "saturation" or richness, and in one case, at least, that of red and green, both may also be of about equal "brightness." Still further aspects of similarity can be indicated. In fact, there is no case of harmony that is a clear exception to the principle of likeness in difference, similarity in the midst of contrast.

If this principle is sound, there are only two ways of failing to achieve harmony—by too little contrast ("insipidity," "monotony"), and too little similarity ("discord," "incoherence," and "chaos"). Since the contrast and the similarity can refer to different "respects" of comparison, there is no need to fall into insipidity in order to avoid chaos. Red is in much greater contrast to green than is gray, but it is also much more like it in that both are "saturated," whereas gray is the zero of saturation. Thus, a vigorous scientific mind is like a vigorous artistic one in that both are "vigorous," even though in almost opposite ways. When, therefore, we say that opposites attract, we must remember that opposites may be all the more alike, in another sense, just by reason of their opposition. We should not say that unlikeness is the cause of attraction, but that the interweaving of pronounced unlikeness with pronounced likeness is the cause of all esthetic attraction and coherence in the world.

A good esthetic maxim is to be bold in the use of contrast. Otherwise, one is likely to avoid discord only upon pain of falling into insipidity. Pronounced contrast gives "strength," "vitality," to art. Besides, if one is timid in the use of contrast, one is hardly sure even of avoiding discord, for scarlet and orange, though less widely contrasting than red and green, are discordant. And the worst musical discords are half-tones. On the other hand, there is a value, connoted by such words as "subtlety," "delicacy," in avoiding contrasts that are too obvious or violent. Yet delicacy at the cost of slight vitality is "effete."

The importance of contrast is not confined to art. All through life run the great contrasts of man and woman, child and adult, joy and sorrow, lively and calm temperaments or moods, etc. Schemes of life which attempt to reduce everything to a uniformity of any kind must be examined to see if they do not threaten the essential vitality of life's harmonies. For instance, it may be a good thing' to have strict economic equality between some groups in society, pure communism—e.g., among monks. But any proposal to universalize strict equality is perhaps a proposal to render life insipid in this respect. It does not, of course, in the least follow that the present very violent inequalities are justified, either with respect to their violence or with respect to their distribution. On the contrary, I believe that capitalism *in its present-day form* is ugly—and doomed. But when a liberal, such as Henry Simons, proposes, as a substitute, a dual or mixed economy consisting partly of vigorous socialization of large industries, and partly of equally vigorous competition between private enterprises[3] he is by many accused of adopting a timid compromise. He is really being bold in his use of contrasts, and there is some presumption that this will enable such a scheme as his, if followed, to produce more vital harmonies. Red is the opposite of green, competition is the opposite of socialization, but the profound and neglected fact is that red harmonizes with green and that competition is in certain respects much more like its opposite, social ownership, than is that miserable intermediate thing, "regulated" non-competitive private monopoly. For both competition and socialized ownership in their best forms afford some assurance of efficiency in the performance of desirable services, both in a genuine sense embody the ideal of liberty, and both are vigorous thoroughgoing methods, whereas private monopoly, however regulated, if really beyond the reach of competing services (fortunately it rarely is), is in essence inefficient, tyrannical, and half-hearted.

Contrast is found not only throughout life but throughout nature as disclosed by science. There is the shift of the electron between energy levels. The shift is sharp, and has a fixed minimal value which measures the least unit of radiant energy emitted by the electron, e.g., a photon of light. The electron does not relieve the monotony of its existence, we might say, merely by shifting its path a little, but rather by shifting it

3. See *Economic Policy for a Free Society*, by Henry Simons, University of Chicago Press, 1948.

enough to achieve a deep contrast between its two successive states. Again, nature avoids monotony by flowing in waves. A calm lake surface is in so far lacking in contrast, but when the wind ruffles this surface, sharply contrasting planes are introduced. We know now that nature carries on all her fundamental operations, not in the manner of an unruffled stream, or an arrow cleaving the air without deviation from its almost rigid trajectory, but in the manner of a stream simultaneously flowing and ruffling in waves. The wave-pattern, which is a simple scheme of repetitive contrast, is all-pervasive in nature. Furthermore, even to this wave pattern itself there is an equally fundamental contrast, the particle pattern or "wave-packet." Waves are, it seems, collected in pellets. Matter is both continuous and discontinuous, a vital harmony, apparently, of these two sharply contrasting aspects. This unity in duality is called in physics "complementarity." There is still another contrast in nature between living matter and dead matter, or between efficient and final causes. A great physicist, Bohr, has suggested that here too we may have complementarity, such that every particle has a living as well as a non-living, a purposive as well as an automatic aspect. This assumption would make it possible to unite physics and biology as perhaps in no other way.

It is also interesting to note that, beginning with Heraclitus twenty-five centuries ago, a number of philosophers have held that the world is a "unity of opposites." But opposite does not mean simply unlike, but rather: emphatically unlike and —in some respect—emphatically alike. For instance, particles and waves are alike in that both involve sharp contrast; the particle with the surrounding "empty" space, and the waves in their divergent planes. To decide whether the world as disclosed by the new physics is really beautiful apart from man it would be necessary to discuss the question with reference to the categories of quality and meaning as well as the category of harmony which is here alone under consideration. But in so far as the new physics pictures nature as a system of complementarities or vital harmonies, it is immeasurably more satisfying esthetically than the old physics, which was full of monotonous continuities, and of unlikenesses not unified by

equally pronounced likenesses, while it was poor in strong
and well-unified contrasts.

It is plain that if likeness in unlikeness can occur among
ideas, as well as among sense qualities, then in so far the phrase
"intellectual beauty" has a meaning. It is also clear that generalization, in which lies the great thrill of intellectual work,
is a finding of likeness where previously only unlikeness was
perceived; and lastly, it is clear that the widest generalizations,
which are the most thrilling of all, are those which unite the
deepest contrasts under a similarity which spans the contrast. Thus, structurally, science and art have a real kinship
in spite of their difference; in saying this we have suggested
how life itself derives beauty from the contrast in unity of
the scientific and artistic activities of man.

A final observation completing this sketch of the theory
of harmony is that in its temporal aspect harmony involves the
contrast between expectation and fulfillment, and that un-
foreseen novelty is as essential as the realization of the foreseen. Expectation is built up partly by rhythm, which combines contrast, such as that between accented and unaccented,
or filled and empty time intervals (silences in music), with
equality in the length of such intervals. But skillful artists do
not neglect to provide the pleasures of surprise furnished by
frequent disappointments of such expectations. As for science,
it used to glory in the idea that if we knew all about the
present, we would foresee all the future. But the moment we
become so familiar with a piece of music that we too definitely
anticipate its future passages we begin to weary of it. Surprise, ignorance of the future, is then, part of the value of
the present. Moreover, science all along has been an excellent
illustration of this. For the great excitement of science has
always consisted in the almost complete impossibility of predicting the future of scientific discovery. Science predicts everything better, we could almost say, than its own future. Surprise is the constant attendant of scientific progress and is
vital to its value. Hence Lessing well said that he would
rather have the search for truth than the complete truth itself. But the new physics suggests that knowledge "complete"
in such a sense as wholly to exclude surprise (or at any rate,

novelty not predictable in terms of law) has no meaning. This suggestion is esthetically pleasing, like nearly all the other features of the new physics. For if scientific law were the rigid thing it was formerly considered to be, then between it and esthetic law there would be a great gulf fixed. There is a law of musical progression, but absolute prediction by that law is too obviously absurd. The future that comes should, for esthetic purposes, be like the future that one could anticipate; but it should also contrast with it. Otherwise the likeness is devitalized and the relationship of present and future is insipid.

The wave-pattern that pervades nature, and the energy-level structure, are examples of temporal contrast that suggest a certain monotony from a long-run point of view. If the crest of the wave has almost forgotten the preceding crest, the contrast with the trough will have vitality. But if there were any memory of the long succession of crests, then the wave-pattern itself would become a monotony calling for contrast. An hypothesis to explain the prevalance of waves is that the life which, by Bohr's generalized complementarity principle, is in the simplest physical individuals who are extremely limited in memory of the past, so that only a few waves or only a few jumps between energy levels would be retained in the present feeling of these individuals. Thus, there would be no feeling of monotony in spite of the myriad repetitions of the wave patterns or of energy states, especially since the "uncertainty principle" suggests that there would be surprise in the details of the movement. Yet if the universe as a whole is living (that is, subject to Bohr's principle) as thinkers have often supposed, though never with such good reason as contemporary thought furnishes; and if, as there are also reasons for holding which cannot be given here, the life of the universe involves memory even of the most distant past, then eventually the repetitions of the patterns disclosed by current physics would call for relief from monotony in new patterns. If the universe as a whole is really beautiful, then even its "laws" must change, however slowly and—to us—imperceptibly. At any rate, in the human community this is what happens; except that here the change is perceptible. Communities that have no means of preserving the art experiences of the past in permanent records may not feel much monotony in repeating them. But the more we know of the past the less are we capable of being satisfied with its mere repetition. Thus, in highly civilized communities fashions succeed each other in rapid succession in spite of the protests of those who are able to avoid discord between past and present only by avoiding all vital contrast between them.

Novelty and freedom are fundamental to life and to all harmony. Even in looking at a picture we have surprises; for we do not grasp the picture all at once, and as we concentrate on one portion we are only partially prepared for what closer scrutiny of the other portions will reveal. Conservatism in its unmitigated form, or, for the long run, even in mitigated forms, is doomed, as is every idea that seeks to evade the consequences of the fact that time is change through and through—except in so far as time itself has a basic structure of past, present, and future, with such and such basic interrelations. These interrelations are expressible in terms of the three categories mentioned at the beginning of this essay, especially, as we have just seen some reason to think, in their esthetic application. The idea of fixed species (ideas less general than categories) has no more secure foundation than the fact that some changes require even greater time spans than geologic ages to become perceptible. (Such greater time spans are called by Whitehead "cosmic epochs.") But it is apparent that even the laws of electronic behavior are only descriptions of the ways of acting of a certain widely distributed species of creature, whose evolution must be vastly slower than that of the more complicated creatures depending upon it, but whose evolution must—on general principles which have been partly explained in the foregoing—be a fact. The truly "immutable laws" of the universe are to be looked for quite elsewhere than in physics, with its arbitrary constants and its inductive method. They are to be sought in the philosophical disciplines, such as esthetics and logic, which do not deal with arbitrary values of such general variables as the idea of contrast, but with these variables in all their generality, and which employ the method of imaginative experiment, which determines not simply what happens but what can intelligibly be conceived, and hence what it is possible should happen.

These are a few of the ways in which all the sciences, together with philosophy, especially esthetic philosophy, are moving towards a new synthesis such as older philosophers could only dimly dream of, but which there is reason to think would give some of them immeasurable delight could they be aware of it, and could they unify—and so harmonize—the immensely vital contrasts which, with all deep similarities, the new view exhibits in comparison to the old.

CHAPTER THREE

ELEMENTS OF TRUTH
IN THE GROUP-MIND CONCEPT

T HE COSMOLOGICAL and religious doctrines with which we are concerned in these essays may be approached from the standpoint of certain problems of psychology and sociology clustering about the conception of the group mind. That the group mind is a myth most readers will probably concede. But myths may be separated from the literal truth by widely varying distances. Moreover, it is easier for men of scientific training to reject a partly fanciful doctrine than to see all the elements of truth it may contain. There may be no "group mind"; yet in the concept there may be facts of which those who deny the group mind are less aware than those who assert it. Still more, there may be facts which neither the partisans nor the opponents of the concept are likely to see unless they rise above the level on which the controversy concerning it ordinarily takes place. So the question which this chapter has to consider is, what elements of truth are contained in, or are, so to say, in the neighborhood of, the idea of the group mind?

Some of these elements are obvious enough. Social scientists do not need to be told that the characters of individuals vary with the characters of the groups to which they belong, or that there is no such thing as the mere individual, conscious of himself as such, to whom membership in one or more groups may be added as a complication. We all recognize that to be a human individual, and to be a member of at least one or two groups of such individuals, are inseparable aspects of one and the same thing. And we all know too that groups may *in a sense* be said to have purposes and ideas, and so in a sense are analogous to human individuals. What is not so obvious is the precise nature and extent of the analogy, and the difference, in this regard, between different types of groups.

Suppose there really were, in the most literal and complete sense, a "group mind," what would this imply? Let us recall that if a group were a super-individual, strictly analogous to its members, then the members would be analogous to the group. Also, if a group can at the same time be an individual, then it is in principle conceivable that what seems at first sight merely an individual is in reality at the same time a group. And thus the closest conceivable analogy between a man and a group of men could obtain only if a man were himself a group whose members resembled men in having "minds of their own." Now a man is indeed a group, namely of cells (also of molecules), and a cell has a quite unmistakable analogy with the whole man, in that both are organisms with a certain unity of action. Moreover, many philosophers and scientists have held or do hold that cells (or molecules or electrons) are psychical as well as physical individuals—even though their freedom of action is not great—that they have something like minds, or at least are sentient creatures, however simply or lowly their mode of sentience. Thus, the human mind on this assumption really is a group mind, if by that is meant a mind, in itself single, which somehow is inclusive of or involved in a collection of lesser minds. Yet this very assumption enables us to see how far short of having a mind of its own is a group composed of human individuals.

It is not simply that the human body involves a nervous system, whereas the human group does not. After all, inasmuch as protozoa digest and oxygenate without stomach or lungs, organisms might be able to feel or perhaps even think without brain or nerves. What is lacking to the human group is not nervous tissue—as Wertheimer remarked, it contains plenty of such tissue, namely that of its own members—but a sufficient degree of integration of the functioning of such tissue. The question is one of unity. It is tempting to reply that unity or integration is a matter of degree, and that instead of saying there is no group mind we should say there is indeed a group mind, but it is not a highly unified one. This temptation should, I think, be resisted. For though there are all degrees of integration of groups, it does not follow that there are all degrees of integration of whole minds belonging to groups. The reason is, in brief, that half a mind, or a half-unified mind, would be worse than no mind at all, and that there is reason to posit a threshold for selfhood or psychic individuality below which there is, not an imperfect or dilute self, but no self at all.

Suppose, for example, that two men having "little in common" form a group for the time being, say while being together in the wilderness, a group characterized chiefly by disharmony. If this group has a mind of its own, it must be a most unhappy one, having a painfully split personality. Now painfully split or multiple personalities occur, but as abnormal states in individuals not condemned by the normal structure of their species, the human race, to such lack of integrity. It is an aspect of this normal integrity that the two personalities in the multiple person are both human personalities, on the level of the group mind, not of the members (the cells); whereas in the case we have above imagined the split would be between two members whose inability to fuse into a higher unity is a reason not for supposing a disunified whole mind but rather for denying any whole mind as inhering in the group. For nature or God to impose upon such a group a single mind not only would at best be torture, but might even. as a lasting arrangement, be impossible, since the whole mind in this case would, it seems, lack any sufficient incentive to exist, and consequently might cease to exist from some equivalent of a "broken heart," that is, from complete discouragement.

Still, it may be thought that some human groups are sufficiently integrated to escape the evil of essential disunity. But how unified is "sufficiently" unified? I suggest as an answer: a group mind is appropriately posited only if the group is approximately as well unified as the better unified of its members. My reason for this seemingly arbitrary principle is simple: if the members are better unified than the group, then either the group has a deficiency or the members have an excess of unity, when conceived as minds. It is, as I have been insisting, not true that degree of unity is an unlimited variable of mind. One man may integrate a much more complex mode of life than another, but any man who fails to balance the complexity of his life by a corresponding power of unification is a sick man, if he continues to be a man at all. Any mind is an integration on some level of complexity. If on a high level, it is a high type of mind. But disintegration is not a matter of level. A frog is as integrated as a man, and may be more so than some men. Disintegration is a matter of danger or destruction.

On the other hand, we know equally well that an excess of unity is destructive of life. Monotony destroys the will to live as surely as do conflict and chaos. Hence, in speaking of an "excess of unity" we are not departing from the testimony of experience. So the conclusion seems to stand that a group mind that was radically less well-unified than its member minds would mean an absurd (or intolerable) monotony in the members or an intolerable disunity in the group.

The general principle is that differences among individuals concern primarily and normally the level of complexity on which unity in variety occurs, or the kinds of data and functions entering into it, rather than the possession or non-possession of a *balance* between unity and variety, or the achievement of a *mean* between monotony and discord. A caged animal can be bored or it can be driven into a conflict of purposes, and the possibility of the two forms of deviation from the normal is due not to the level of complexity of the animal but to its being a single psychological individual.

The foregoing might be called a principle of basic goodness in nature. Individuals may suffer from tedium or chaos, but no species is specifially inclined toward either extreme. If it were, it would probably not long survive, or it would evolve quickly away from the defect in question.

The law of balance between unity and variety, or of the *equal integrity of all species* has been obscured by a confusion between physiological and psychological standpoints. There are physical "organisms" of all degrees of looseness of organization. If we suppose a simple "parallelism" of physical and psychical, then it would follow that there are all degrees of looseness in psychical integration. The fallacy lies in this, that whereas a physical individual (i.e., an entity taken in its merely spatio-temporal characters) is made *one* individual, one unit of reality, by virtue of some purpose of the observer in carving out that much of his environment and treating it as a single object of thought and behavior, a psychical individual is itself in some sense an observer and has its own unity of purpose, objective to the purposes of its observers. Psychical individuals are self-individuated; they actively distinguish themselves from their environment. It is a matter of convenience where we declare a mountain to end and the next mountain, or the earth's crust beneath, to begin; moreover, the mountain may be regarded as a mass of crystals each exerting force upon all the others, but none of them subject to force exerted by the mountain as anything additional to all the crystals. In contrast, a man cannot reasonably, and by himself he cannot possibly, be regarded as merely a system of cells acting upon one another, for he is directly aware of "himself" as, at the given moment, a single unit of action, a single mind or will, exerting force upon his bodily parts and thence upon the world. When he thinks or wills, it is not any one or any number of his cells that thinks his thoughts or wills his purposes, but himself as an irreducible unit, as much a unit as any cell or any atom or any electron. To be sure, some scientists have verbally "believed" that they themselves were simply their cells or their particles acting in interrelated fashion, but it is intuitively plain, to me at least, that no one can mean by himself anything less (in any one moment) than a single unit of action, the only one indeed which is directly experienced with much insistence or distinctness. Analysis will show that if this intuition is denied the upshot is that no unit of action whatever can be known.

The point is not merely that the man as such has a certain unity, and is not just a group of cells or atoms or electrons; the point is further that the man is *as much* a single dynamic unit as is any of his parts. As Leibniz put it, the human personality is the dominant monad in the society of monads constituting "his body," which is defined as his by this dominance relation. (Of course, we need not accept all Leibniz's doctrines concerning the nature of monads; especially should we reject his denial that monads literally interact.) Now there is no reason why every society of monads should have a radically dominant member. Some societies are "democracies." Whitehead says this is true even of a tree or other many-celled plant, and botanists do in fact incline to conceive a tree as a colony of plant cells which have individually more unity than the whole they compose. It is therefore not necessary to accept a "vegetative" soul or dominant monad for the plant as a whole. Leibniz was admirably cautious here, in that he expressed doubt as to whether a plant is a dynamic unit. Any unit of action of the plant may, in fact, be conceived as due entirely to the cells (and molecules and the like), as affecting each other, on the one hand, and to the general unity of nature (and perhaps God) on the other.

Of course, the plant is not, as the Gestaltists say, a mere "and-sum" of the cells, if this refers to the cells as each would be if it existed elsewhere than in the plant colony. Outside the colony the cells could not be entirely the same; but neither could a tree be the same if the trees or the soil around it were different. Yet in this lies no more reason for considering the tree a dynamic unit than for supposing the tree and its near surroundings to be such a unit. It is the general unity of the universe which makes it impossible that anything should remain internally just what it is when its environment is altered. The question of a dominant monad or "soul," however, is a question not merely of unity but of *individual* unity, unity whose boundaries from other things are no less important than the internal boundaries of its parts, and whose mode of coherence within these boundaries is distinctive and sharply contrasted to the mode extending beyond them. The relation between two branches of a tree is a crude mechanical relation compared to that between different parts of a plant cell. The tree pipes supplies to both branches and supports both from falling; but the different parts of a cell are bound together with far greater intimacy and subtlety. In the vertebrate body, to be sure, there is a similar piping of supplies, but there is also, controlling their flow (as the least of its functions), a nervous system the virtue of which is that it enables a many-celled creature to possess a unity which is in many places at once, acting on, and receiving influences from, the cells, and irreducible to their action on one another.

To call a tree an organism may serve for physiological purposes, since natural selection operates to produce such cooperation of parts as tends to preserve the whole, regardless of whether or not this cooperation is in some degree due to the control of the parts by a super or group mind, a dominant monad. From this point of view, which is prominent in biology, a tree really is a single organism, a unit of survival and of struggle for existence. But from the standpoint of psychology, no matter how generalized, a plant colony is probably only a pseudo-organism, though its member cells may be genuine organisms.

Our question is whether a human group is essentially a democracy—a colony of organisms lacking radical unity and therefore without a dominant monad, lacking, that is, a full-fledged group mind that disposes of the members for its own purposes—or whether it is so unified that it can as a whole possess a single individual mind, metaphysically speaking the aristocrat, or super-member, of the group. Consider the manner in which Americans influence one another within the United States. Is it not essentially the same as the manner in which they influence persons in other countries? Information, ideas, expressions of sentiment, are pumped about by the same basic means of press, radio, travel, personal contact, whether American is acting on American, or American is acting on Englishmen or even on Russians. The boundary between this country and Canada seems hardly analogous to the skin separating one nervous system from another. A religious body, or family ties, might unite members of both countries as intimately as anything unites persons of the same country. Not that national unity is not a powerful force, a truly terrible force even, but that it seems in principle accounted for by the same sort of connections as unite human beings with other human beings generally, these connections having certain especially intensive effects where geographic and historic continuity is pronounced and results in political unity. To add the idea of a dominant monad to this picture is of questionable aid in understanding it, and is practically certain to lead to false inferences. A hurricane is an awe-inspiring and terrifying force, but it is not an organism or primary dynamic unit of nature. Human beings must look to some group for security, and for certain important purposes the national group is naturally chosen. All this follows and is intelligible quite without the supposition that the nation is a super-*individual* which thinks and wills its own destiny.[1]

The unity of the family is similarly intelligible without supposing that the family, or a married couple, has a mind of its own. The "we" in this case assuredly and profoundly affects the "I," but it does not follow that the we is a super-I.

It may, to be sure, be vaguely imaginable that a nation has purposes which transcend those of any of its members, somewhat as human purposes surpass any that could be entertained by bodily cells. But what is explained by this supposition that could not better be explained otherwise? Not merely would such a super-purpose be beyond our understanding; it would mean that there must be a deliberate purpose in the blundering and often catastrophic behavior of a given nation (such as, perhaps, this country thinking, for a time at least, that it could win a war without fighting it, or that it could wisely run the risk of being forced into a war after it had permitted all possible allies to be destroyed), behavior exhibiting all the marks of well-known forms of human ignorance and weakness, rather than of unknown forms of superhuman awareness. The inability of human beings to grasp and courageously face the fearful complexities of international affairs except by heroic efforts, and in brief and rare periods, seems a more promising reason for recent national behavior than any notion that in some superhuman way each nation as a unit knows what it is doing, or at least thinks it does.

The foregoing argument as it stands appears to exclude all purpose higher than the human from the factors operating in

---

1. An excellent discussion of this will be found in Ernest Barker's introduction to his translation of Gierke's *Natural Law and the Theory of Society* (Cambridge, Eng., 1934) vol. 1, pp. xxviii-xxxiv. (I owe this reference to Dr. Leo Strauss.)

history. But it is one thing to impute self-individuality to a national group, and another to impute it to some much more inclusive whole. Such a more inclusive whole might be the human race, or the planet with all its contents, or the stellar system, or—to my mind most credibly of all—the entire universe. Such a super-national mind would not have to be held guilty of the misconduct of nations. For it might be conceived as leaving the conduct of nations to be determined by their members, while reserving for itself the maintenance of a more comprehensive order by which national action would be made possible and kept within limits. The assumption could be, and I think should be, that freedom is essential to man, if not to all beings, freedom from complete control even by a higher order of being, so that it is better that men be allowed to blunder into a certain amount of catastrophe than that they be deprived of all power over matters of importance, of all large scope and initiative. If, however, we try to conceive of a nation as a self-active individual, it will not be easy to assign it a function that will leave to the members of the nation the power of political choice and responsibility which members, particularly of advanced nations, feel is theirs. To deny the correctness of this feeling is to do great harm to man on his political and eventually on his nonpolitical, side. What always happens is that in the nations which claim to possess a group super-mind the political choices are made not by this super-mind but by a small group, or an individual, coercing the remainder. The boasted transcendence of individualism is really, as is well known, one of the worst possible forms of egoistic individualism, individualism for the few, and they by no means the most public spirited.

It might, in spite of all this, be true that each nation has in a fashion a purpose of its own, in somewhat the sense in which a hand has its function in the purpose of the whole body. To God or some super-national mind each nation may be a sort of organ, and the embodiment of a purpose. But this is a purpose which it serves, not a purpose which it entertains as its own. The mind which entertains this purpose will sway the actions of one nation only as it also sways those of other nations (beyond the limits assigned to human freedom) . In this it will perform a function which cannot be left to man, because it concerns affairs too vast for human understanding or control. A mind able to understand and control England, for example, in superhuman fashion should be able to understand humanity as well, since there are many non-Englishmen who know more about the political problems of England than most Englishmen, showing that a higher level of mind could hardly limit itself to a single nation as constituting its body, its sphere of primary activity. It is hard enough for an intelligent statesman to feel content with the limitations of his nationality. How much harder for a superior mind to be shut up to the functions of the group mind of a nation!

Personally, I do not see much to be said (if there is anything, Fechner said it) for any group mind above the human individual and below the mind of the entire cosmos. If the cosmic community has a group mind, the sole nonlocalized one, it can hardly be denied that this mind has functions which could not otherwise be discharged, at least by a mind. Men may guide the affairs of their nation, but they certainly do not guide the affairs of the universe. No human thought produced (in spite of Kant's verbal belief that a sort of unconscious human thought did produce) the cosmic pattern of laws and things obeying these laws. From this pattern are derived the basic conditions of human life, which, together with human freedom, explain human history. We do not by taking thought bring it about that we live in a cosmos, though we do by taking thought have appreciable effects, at least upon the fashion in which our environment continues to include our own nation. The cosmic functions are as clearly superhuman as the national functions are human. The latter represent man both in some of his worst and in some of his best aspects; the former in their basic pattern exhibit nothing either of human vice or of human virtue.

That a nation goes on while the individual disappears is true, but no more true than that a forest goes on while its trees die, or that a river goes on while its molecules are lost to it, or that humanity goes on while nations disappear, or that the planet goes on, perhaps after all men have vanished from its surface. The on-going of nations is at least partly due to the conscious human purpose that they should go on, men actually dying, and not infrequently or in small numbers, for this express end. And what is not due to human purpose here may be due to a will far above the merely national level. The heart goes on as a heart as long as the man, though not because there is a heart-will but because the heart cells, on the one hand, and the whole body (and nature as a whole) on the other, unconsciously or consciously tend toward this end. Similarly, the nation may be an organ rather than an organism.

The assumption of a super-national mind, whether cosmic or not, has great pragmatic advantages. It enables us to avoid the dangerous if not absurd conception of the human being as the summit of the scale of beings. This conception is really much more absurd than is sometimes realized, for it means that there are many summits of being, many "Supreme Beings," and this in turn implies an awkward dilemma. Either the Supreme Beings take account of one another's interests only on the principle of fair exchange, or mutual profit, or they consider themselves as bound by sympathy to the interests of others—ultimately, and this is the sole rationally possible criterion, to the interests of all, or of the greatest number. But either conception leads to difficulties.

We cannot account for moral obligation on the exchange or mutual profit principle. For example, we have obligations to posterity, which nevertheless can do nothing for us in return. ("What has posterity done for us?" someone has asked.) And the psychological fact is that every man lives in at least some slight degree for others as well as for himself, which means that he implicitly views himself as contributing to some whole of value of which his own satisfactions are only a part. The fact of death makes this the only rational view for him to take, as sympathey makes it the only consistently practicable one. To suppose that each man lives only for the sake of his own enjoyment while alive implies that his own death is for him the absolute evil, at least if death means the total destruction of one's enjoyment, and—at least if there is no superhuman mind—why should it not mean that? Yet who lives or could live as though his death were absolute evil? To say that we live partly to enjoy our sympathies for others is to say that we live for the sake of living for others, which is a cumbersome way of saying that we live in at least some degree for the sake of others, which is the point at issue.

The confusion, of which many philosophers have been guilty, is due, like many philosophical errors, to neglecting the temporal aspect of the problem, in this case the temporal structure of interest. (See Chapter Five) The enjoyment of planning the welfare of others, as in making a benevolent will, is an enjoyment that occurs when the will is made and while the individual lives. But the future goal of the act is primarily the welfare of the legatees, which one may expect to outlast one's own enjoyment of the will-making or its results by many years. To deny that one ever makes the will for the sake of others will lead by the same logic to the denial that any act is done for the sake of the future. All action is self-enjoyed, but its *future* goal is not by any means always self-enjoyment. The simple truth is that long run self-interest is no more inevitable than is some measure, however limited, of altruism. As Whitehead has profoundly said, the self is a "society" of past and future experiences bound together by a mode of sympathy which, in a specifically different but generically similar way, unites us also to the experiences belonging to the temporal societies constituting other personalities. The self, in other words, is a *temporal group mind* as well as a spatial one. It focuses, in its present, what it knows of experiences belonging to other selves as well as experiences in its own past and future

But if we live for the sake of others—ultimately, so far as we are rational, for the sake of all selves, or of the most inclusive group we can effectively serve—the question arises, can this be intelligible if the group is merely that, merely a set of interrelated selves? A collection does not literally have interests that can be satisfied. What is it that makes the sum of human values itself a value, and the all-inclusive value? The included values are concrete enjoyments, satisfactions, but the "satisfaction of many," or of all, is not itself a satisfaction in the same concrete literal sense, unless there be an individual who *takes* satisfaction in the being-satisfied of all. In an abstract theoretical way every man, upon reflection, wishes all men to be satisfied, but the next man he meets concretely he may wish sadistically to see in torment; and certainly he cannot concretely and fully enjoy the enjoyments of even his nearest neighbors. The only way to avoid a certainly false, purely self-interest theory of motivation, and at the same time do justice to the principle that value lies in concrete individual satisfaction, not in mere collections, is to recognize a superhuman mind. If this include the sum of being, if it be the cosmic mind, then the problem is solved, since such a mind would indeed find satisfaction in the satisfactions of all, for all would be integral parts of its own body, whose health would be inseparable from the prevailing health of its parts.

A merely national super-mind, on the other hand, would only set up *between nations* the problem of self-interest versus abstract collectivism. And even a mind of the human race would not entirely solve the problem. To *concretize* the idea of the good of all, the super-mind must be omniscient, at least so far as the field of human experience is concerned. But theologians and philosophers would probably almost all agree that omniscience must be cosmic or nothing. There are many cells in the human body which do not effectively contribute to the enjoyment of the human mind, and this is because a localized mind cannot be localized altogether sharply, since the universe is universally interactive. To be ignorant of part of what is going on outside one's body is to be partially ignorant even of what is going on inside it.

If the ultimate value is an enjoyment inclusive of all enjoyments, and if the ultimate motive is to enhance the ultimate value by contributing our own enjoyment, and that of all those we can help, to this inclusive enjoyment, then there is no mystery in our ability to work even for the sake of posterity, which can make no return to us but will certainly make a return to the ultimate value. Thus, my contention is that the idea of a group mind is valuable and sound, though in application to a merely human group it is probably false and certainly dangerous.

And it is as necessary to avoid denying that human minds enter into or contribute to the life of a higher mind as it is to avoid asserting that this higher mind is localized upon the planet. Traditional religious ideas are somewhat ambiguous in relation to this problem. Ten thousand times over, God has been defined as totally "independent" of human beings, creating them and giving them all things, but receiving from them nothing in return. In such definitions God is not at all the cosmic group mind. I firmly believe that if religion is to perform its function of furnishing the supreme perspective for all values, it must outgrow the crudity of this purely one-way relation between creator and creature. Man has an ultimately *rational* need to regard himself as contributing to something quite as concrete and individual as himself, but, unlike himself, not limited and localized in space and time (nor yet, for all that, purely timeless and immaterial!). If religion persists in telling us that God is eternally complete and self-sufficient in all respects, so that no contribution of any kind can be made to the divine experience, then men will look elsewhere for the concrete meaning of the "good of all" or the common good. But where shall they find it? Obviously in some dangerous myth or a non-divine group mind.

It may seem an objection to the foregoing to remark that men such as Hitler have been known to appeal to God, and apparently a God of "nature" and so, presumably, of the cosmos.

My comment is that the cosmos is not altogether an open book, and that the interpretation of the cosmic mind is not a matter concerning which a busy dictator is to be supposed a high authority, or concerning which he may not talk lies or nonsense as readily as in more humble matters. In interpreting the mind of the cosmic community a man has two chief aids, of neither of which have the dictators, presumably, made much use. One is the religious tradition and experience, that is, the deposit and living continuation of intuitions of the depths of life where relations to God may be felt and enacted; and the other is metaphysical inquiry and its history. Unfortunately metaphysics was sidetracked for two millennia by an insufficiently exact, insufficiently analytic, conception of God as the "absolute," the "perfect," the "complete" or "self-sufficient" or "independent" being. This conception was involved in antinomies (See Chapter Six) and, as I have suggested above, does not meet the concrete religious need. Is this not an invitation to semi-insane or malicious persons to conceive God not only as not perfect in the impossible metaphysical sense but as imperfect in just that all-too-human sense which will render him subservient to their designs?

The "group mind" in the bad sense was the result of the common failure of atheism and traditional absolutistic theism to furnish any rational conception of a concrete whole to which we can devote ourselves and which, by this devotion, we can enrich with a value that it would otherwise lack. Thus, men were condemned to live for themselves, or for one another as together constituting a collection without concrete inclusive unity, the entire collection being apparently doomed to extinction when the planet ceases, some day, to be habitable. Thus, there was, it seemed, no relevant common measure of value, and no permanent treasury of achievement. Men were separate entities, but infinitely far from any kind of self-sufficiency. From these absurdities atheism cannot escape without myth, and theism cannot escape without equivocation unless it unlearns its too simple and blind rejection of pantheism and panentheism, its rejection of the concrete or group mind conception of God.[2] No doubt this conception is only an "analogy," or, if you prefer, the cosmic group mind is an infinitely special or unique case of group mind; but the concept conveys an element of truth which the usual analogies fail to render equally explicit.

In sum, there is reason to think that the unity to which human purposes are contributory extends vertically too deep to be cut horizontally by national or other human boundaries. And this is important for the whole problem of human freedom, for if the nation be taken as the super-whole, then the human individual is reduced in value to his political aspect; only what can be effective for national action exists in the final reckoning. True, it cannot be proved that the unknown national mind is unaffected by even the most private individual thoughts. But the significance of the private and personal becomes radically uncertain if the national mind is taken

---

2. One of the first to understand this was G. T. Fechner; see the chapter on "God and the World" in his *ZendAvesta*. For a recent instance see W. P. Montague, *The Ways of Things* (New York, 1941), Chapter 6.

mystically; and it becomes drastically curtailed if the national mind is identified with all that can definitely be known of it, the national group behavior. It is self-evident that at best the national mind cannot embrace the entire private life of each man, since only omniscience can do that. States can be expected to grant adequate freedom to the private life only if the significance of this life be taken to transcend the nation— not because the part is more than the whole, a manifest absurdity, but because the whole of which man is finally a part, or the whole of which the *whole man* is a part, is not the nation but that which transcends the nation in space and time as the nation transcends the man, and at the same time (and here was what Hegel overlooked) transcends the nation in concreteness and integrity as the man transcends the nation.

Only when it is seen that *the relations of superiority between man and nation run in both directions,* and when it is seen that man's unequivocal superior must be something which is also unequivocally superior to the nation (or any human group) can the relations of man to his group be treated with the proper perspective, avoiding the twin evils of abstract individualism and abstract (or mythically organic) collectivism.

CHAPTER FOUR

A SYNTHESIS OF IDEALISM
AND REALISM

IN DISCUSSIONS of "idealism" and "realism," two very different questions have often been confused or, when distinguished, still not correctly and clearly related to each other. One is the question, how fundamental and universal in reality is "mind," "soul," or "experience," in general and as such? This is the ontological question. The other question is epistemological. When a given subject knows something, "its object," does the former depend on the latter, or the latter on the former, or are the two mutually interdependent? The idealists are accused by realists of the following procedure: from an untenable answer to the epistemological question, they seek to derive the idealistic answer to the ontological question. My contentions are, that the realists have been largely right, and the idealists often largely wrong, concerning the epistemological question, but that *both* realists and idealists have in most cases been largely wrong as to the logical relations between this question and the ontological one. For I hold that the realistic position in epistemology is the very one from which the most cogent argument for an idealistic ontology can be derived.

It must be understood that by "subject," in this chapter, is meant anything that can be said to be aware of (know or feel or intuit) anything. The concept is intended in a radically broad and non-anthropomorphic sense. Fish presumably have a sort of awareness; but this awareness is surely not "human." There may be inhabitants of some other planet who enjoy awareness, again certainly not human awareness. Finally, deity, if there be any meaningful idea of it, involves some supremely excellent form of awareness or realization, radically other than the essentially defective, fallible, partial, localized-body-bound awareness that alone can reasonably be ascribed to us *anthropoi*.

It is also to be understood that by "subject" is not meant ego, soul, personality, or "spiritual substance." The same ego or person may (today) be unaware of object O and (tomorrow) be aware of it. Thus, it is not the ego *simpliciter* that is aware of O, but the ego in a certain "state." Now, as we are using language, a "subject" is something that *simpliciter* or by definition is aware of something, something determinate or unequivocal. It is the subjective "pole" of an actual subject-object relation. Thus the state, not the substance, the experience (in its aspect of awareness *of* something) not the ego, is the subject. Descartes may not have proved that he existed as substance or permanent ego, but he did prove, if anything can be proved, that there are momentary experiences. These experiences, as being *of* something, as having objects, are the "subjects" of this article—except when the distinction between enduring person and momentary experience is irrelevant to the argument.

Consider then the following four theses:—

1. An "object," or that of which a particular subject is aware, in no degree depends upon that subject.

Principle of *Objective Independence*.

Common sense, Aristotle, Moore, Perry, Whitehead.

2. A "subject," or whatever is aware of anything, always depends upon the entities of which it is aware, its objects.

Principle of *Subjective Dependence*.

Common sense, Aristotle, Whitehead.

(1) and (2) constitute "realism."

3. Any entity must be (or at least be destined to become) object for *some* subject or other.

Principle of *Universal Objectivity*. "Idealism."

Berkeley, Whitehead.

4. Any concrete entity is a subject, or set of subjects; hence, any other concrete entity of which a subject, S1, is aware, is another subject or subjects (S2; or S2, S3, etc.)

Principle of *Universal Subjectivity*. "Panpsychism."

Leibniz, Peirce, Whitehead.

The doctrine of this chapter is that these four principles are not in conflict or competition with each other, but are rather complementary or mutually supporting. The theory which asserts all four principles as forming a coherent unity may be called, with Whitehead, "reformed subjectivism"; also "societism," for it amounts to a social theory of reality.

That (1) and (2) are harmonious with each other seems fairly evident. (1) provides the subject with something to know; (2) declares that this knowledge conforms to the known. Thus, truth by correspondence is grounded. Facts exist; by submitting to their influence upon us we know these facts correctly. We are thus molded to the things, not the things to us (apart from fictions).

What are the relations of (1) and (3)? Berkeley and others have given the impression that the idealistic argument runs: what we know is our idea, hence dependent on us, hence everything knowable is mind dependent. But even Berkeley himself presumably did not believe that when he knew his friends they became his ideas in such fashion as made them *ipso facto* dependent upon him; or that when he studied Plato (or knew God) this caused Plato (or God) to become dependent for existence upon Bishop Berkeley! And indeed, objective independence (1) is logically compatible with universal objectivity (3). The first states that relation to a particular subject knowing an entity is extrinsic to that entity; the second states that relation to subjectivity in general is not thus extrinsic. There is no contradiction in combining these assertions; just as no logical difficulty opposes combining, "John must wear some garment rather than none" with "There is no necessity for John to wear this coat" (rather than some other garment). That an entity could be precisely itself were it unknown to S1, or were it unknown to S2, or to any subject you choose to point out, does not imply it could be itself were it unknown to anyone, were it simply unknown. Consider an ambitious man who feels that he could not stand existence as a "mere nobody," without fame or prestige. It does not follow that he could not stand existence if precisely I or you were unaware of his claims to praise. He wants an audience, but any audience with suitable characteristics will do. Similarly, idealism holds that entities need to be known, but that any subject suitable for the function of knowing the given entity will suffice. Or consider the relations of fish to water. Some water or other they must have, but there is no one body of water rather than another which is required. Perhaps being-known is to entities in general what water is to fish.

An objection to the foregoing might be that it makes at least some difference to the ambitious man just what his audience is, and some difference to fish in what body of water they are placed. Let us then take another analogy. According to the Aristotelian theory of universals or forms, there can be no forms (apart from fictitious *combinations* of forms) apart from individual substances. Without men no humanity, without dogs no caninity, etc. But there could be humanity without Socrates, or without any man or men you choose to mention. And it would be the *same* universal or generic form. For this is the meaning of universality: that it is neutral to individual differences. Why may we not regard X-is-known-by-someone-or-other as a universal, and X-is-known-*by*-S1 as an individual case of this universal? Then the Aristotelian principle would be that X-is-known does not in the least depend upon S1; for any other subject-knowing-X would do. Yet X-is-known does depend upon there being *some* suitable subject enjoying X as its object. And it follows that if X depends upon or is inseparable from X-is-known, it still might be absolutely independent of S1, just as "humanity" is absolutely independent of Socrates, though not of there being *some* suitable concrete instances or other.

Return again to the ambitious man. Suppose the fame that he requires is posthumous fame. He needs, then, to believe that posterity will remember him. Here no individuals as such are intrinsic to his state of mind. Only the generic "some individuals or other (in suitable numbers and of suitable intelligence or worth) remembering X with praise or gratitude" is involved. Here we have a universal allowing for innumerable variations of individual embodiment. Yet the universal calls for some embodiment if the ambition is to be satsfied. Now, perhaps there is in "being" a sort of ambition to be remembered, to be made use of in subsequent occurrences, an ambition which must be satisfied. We shall see that this is less fantastic than might appear at first thought.

What has been shown so far is that (3) is compatible with (1) and (2). The same can be said of (4), the principle of panpsychism. If what I know is another subject, it may still be true that in this knowing I depend upon that other subject, while it does not depend upon me. The biographer of Washington apparently has his mental life to a considerable extent molded by the experiences of Washington which he studies, but there is no evidence that Washington's experiences were molded by any future biographer. (Naturally, a given man's belief about Washington is determined in part by his own nature; but this belief is merely about Washington, not identical with him.) Panpsychism may thus be a wholly "realistic" doctrine, if realism is defined through (1) and (2).

It appears, then, that the idealistic interpretation of reality as essentially relative to or consisting of mind, experience, awareness, that is, either Berkeleyan or panpsychic idealism, is entirely compatible with a realistic view of the independence of the particular object and the dependence of the particular subject, in each subject-object situation. It may also be urged that we need the word "realism" to refer to the mere thesis that an act of knowledge must be derivative from a known which is not derivative from that act. Thus, the practice of contrasting "idealism" and "realism," as though they were contradictories, is of doubtful convenience. "Realistic idealism," or "realistic subjectivism," has a reasonable and consistent meaning.

I wish now to contend that not only are the realistic theses compatible with idealism, but that they furnish a basis for a cogent idealistic argument. Only certain steps in the argument can here be set forth.

Any actual occurrence, once it occurs, immediately acquires the status of being past. Past always means, past for some new present, some new occurrence. What is this relation of being-past, or of having-as-past? Such a relation is given whenever an event is remembered. Memory is at least *a* way of being past, or of having-as-past. What other ways, if any, can be pointed to? One may say, the cause is past for the effect, or the effect has the cause as its past, its predecessor in time. But then what is this relation of causality? And let us bear in mind that the answer must derive from some given instance. We are at Hume's problem. Is there a convincing non-idealistic answer? Whitehead, James, Bergson, Kant, and others have "answered Hume," but these answers are all in psychological terms, essentially within idealism in the broadest sense of (3) and (4). For the rest Hume, so far as I see, has not really been answered. Again, suppose one drops "causality," and merely says that "pastness," or "before" and "after," are ultimate data of experience. We hear one note as "after" another, and that is all there is to it. But still, is it possible to separate, as an experienced datum, "B comes after A," from "when B is heard, A is remembered"? We are at Kant's problem of distinguishing subjective and objective succession. But Kant did not exhaust the possible solutions. An objective serial order does not require that there be a strictly deterministic causal relation, an invariant "rule" according to which precisely B is bound to follow once A has occurred. Suppose there is a relation of B to A, intrinsic to B but extrinsic to A. Thus "A occurs" would not entail "B occurs"; but "B occurs" would entail "A has occurred" since B, according to the hypothesis, involves a relation to A requiring A as *relatum*. But how is such a relation to be conceived concretely? The only positive answer furnished by experience is memory. If B remembers A, while A is unaware of B, then the objective order of the two must be: A by itself, not involving B, then B-remembering-A. If all reality is some form of experience, with each unit endowed with some form of memory, then an objective temporal order is explicable. If I observe you to smile and then to frown, this order of events is in my experience as, first, a perception of smiling without reference to frowning, and second, a perception of frowning referring to smiling as its remembered antecedent. In your experience there is the same order, since you too in feeling yourself to frown have a sense of having just smiled. For an experience B to "follow" A is an intrinsic property of B. This property is memory in its basic or "pure," aspect (Bergson). It is not equally true that for an experience A to "precede" B is an intrinsic property of A. For the creative aspect of experience lies in the fact that it is never literally anticipated. Abstract general features are anticipated, but not particular experiences as such. On the other hand, psycho-analysis lends some support to the Bergsonian-Whitehead thesis that memory refers not to abstract features but to particular events in their particularity. And there are other grounds for the thesis.

The foregoing considerations suggest that one dimension of reality, the temporal, is best conceived as the memory-creativity structure of experience as such. The present experience is as subject with past experience as its object; in this subject-object relation, the particularity of the past experience (the object) is intrinsic to the present experience (the subject), while the particularity of the present experience is extrinsic to that of the past. The two realistic theses are thus observed. But also, one may hold, the object is bound to be remembered by *some* future experience or other; and indeed, while no experience anticipates particular successors, experiences do, at least normally, involve a sense that they will be looked back upon by some sort of memory.

The logic of the foregoing argument is nearly the reverse of what idealistic logic has generally been supposed to be. Whereas the realist urges the independence of the known and the dependence or relativity of the knower, the idealist is supposed to urge the dependence of the known and the independence or "absoluteness" of the knower—at least of some one knower, such as God. But it is, rather, the relativity of the subject that should incline us to idealism. Modern logic should by this time have cured us of the absurd prejudice that, to explain everything, the great thing is to find the nonrelative, or absolute. On the contrary, not nonrelation is our main problem, but relation, a world of structural order. And nothing can constitute this but something that can intrinsically have relation, be genuinely relative. A subject, according to realism, is just such an intrinsically relative entity, in its very nature more or less conformed to something not itself. The subject is rich in relations, the mere object has no relation, at least not to the particular subject which has it as object. But, the reader may object, it is the effect that is relative, the cause that is self-sufficient or absolute, and it is the cause that explains things, not the effect. However, please observe that every cause, with the problematic exception of God, is also effect; further, that unless we can understand what it is to be an effect we shall certainly not understand what it is to be cause. Subjects, experiences, are certainly effects, since memory is clearly a result of the thing remembered (perhaps along with other causes). But since the thing remembered is itself an experience, in this case, at least, both cause (or part of it) and effect are subjects. And here we see the relational structure that so much controversy over idealism seems to have missed. That subject S-1 is relative to object O-1 is quite compatible with O-1's being itself another subject, S-2, itself relative to another object, O-2, this object itself a third subject, S-3, etc. It is effects that, in other relations, are also causes; it is the dependent and relative that, in another relation, is independent or absolute;[1] likewise, it is subjects that, in other subject-object relations, are also objects, things known. In memory, experiences are both subjects and objects; each is subject for its predecessors and object for its successors. But since it is the subject that is intrinsically relative, or really has the subject-object relation, to say of a thing that it is subject is genuinely to describe it, while to say of something that it is object for a certain subject is to describe only the subject, since the asserted relationship belongs exclusively to it. Thus, in the idea of subject, that of object is fully embraced. In principle, materialism can add nothing to panpsychic description of reality. It cannot add relativity; for the subject is relative to its object. It cannot add nonrelativity or independence; for since subject can be object (for other subjects), and since by (1) it must then, in that relation, be independent, it follows that subjects can, so far as certain relations are concerned, be nonrelative. Since subjects can be effects, they can certainly be causes; for every effect is cause of subsequent effects. In the subject-object relation, interpreted pan-

---

1. It may be asked, must there not be something that, in *all* relations, is absolute? My answer to this question will be found in my book, *The Divine Relativity* (Yale University Press, 1948). It is there held that there must be something universally non relative or absolute, but that this something is not simply identical with the Supreme Being or with God, and is no actual subject.

psychically, we have precisely the "asymmetrical transitive relations" that modern logic has discovered to be fundamental in reality. The memory of the memory of the memory of A is memory of A; but A is not memory of the memory of the memory of A. The relation runs one way only, but it is transitive. Surely a principle thus illustrated in experience is worth two or a million verbally formulated principles for which a single illustration in the given is lacking. "Matter" is one of the other million; for whoever directly intuited a bit of matter as intrinsically referring to its past? Only experience as such exhibits this intrinsic relativity.

I submit that, if we put aside medieval (theological) prejudices which exalt the "absolute," we shall see that the one-sided relativity which realism finds in the subject-object relation is reason for expecting the subject as such to prove explanatory of the nature of things.

It is unnecessary to explain in detail how the panpsychic principle is to be reconciled with the doctrines of physics, since this task has been performed by Whitehead—especially in *Science and the Modern World* and in *Process and Reality*. I mention only that one must generalize the notion of "memory" to include not only cases where the remembered experience expresses the same personality or ego, but also those in which this is not the case. For example, we remember feelings which have just been felt by the bodily cells, without for all that being distinctly aware of the individual cells as such. Whitehead has shown how "extension" as well as temporal succession can be decribed in panpsychic terms.

The panpsychic principle is able to remove the air of paradox that otherwise clings to the Berkeleyan principle. It may seem nothing to a stone that there are (or will be) subjects aware of the stone. But if the stone consists of subjects, the matter is altered. For each of us is most anxious, painfully so at times, to call the attention of other subjects to ourselves, that is to get them to make us their objects. The full exploration of this topic would take us into the philosophy of religion, in which it would be shown that our very being is our sense of presence to the divine subject.[2] We should also have to meet the objection that the divine subject must be conceived as wholly "absolute," whereas we have held that every subject is, in relation to its objects, relative or derivative. Our answer would be a theory of the divine as both absolute and relative, in diverse aspects. This would not contradict the principle of subjective dependence or relativity; since *qua* actual subject with given objects, the divine would be relative, and its absoluteness would qualify only an abstract "character" within this subject (or rather, series of subjects).[2]

The case for panpsychic idealism can be summarized as follows:

1. In the subject we have a really connected or genuinely relative, "internally related," term. Human subjects furnish examples; but what principle of relativity can be found in the idea of "concretes that are simply not subjects"? What in a present actuality refers back to the past, what *in* anything is the objective counterpart of what we conceive as "its" history? The leaf resting on the ground "has fallen" there, but this having-fallen, where is it, as property of the leaf, or of anything else? In our memory (real or imagined), our past experience (real or imagined) of the leaf may inhere as a feature of present experience. But that is no help to the anti-idealist, who must find another objective meaning for "past" as a real relation of something. It comes down to this. Things either intrinsically refer to, "take account of" other things, for example, past events, or they internally contain no such reference to other things. Or, in other words, there either is self-reference to other actuality, or there is not. If there is such reference, then it is at least *as if* the thing perceived or remembered or felt the other. For "taking account of" is the external or spectator's indication of what internally to the thing itself can only be imagined as perception or feeling or memory. And if, to take the other horn of the dilemma, there is no self-reference of one thing to another, then the world has no real connectedness, and is no world, no real succession of cause-effect, at all. Thus, it is analytic that either everything must be as if idealism (panpsychism) were true, or else as if there were no world, no

<hr>

2. *Ibid.* Also see my article, "Ideal Knowledge Defines Reality," *Journal of Philosophy*, Vol. XLIII, pp. 573-82.

real temporal-causal system. Positivism and panpsychic idealism exhaust the positions that have any semblance of clear
meaning. And of the two it is idealism that alone makes sense
when considered with reference to the deeper intellectual and
other needs of man. There is a world, a temporal-causal process,
and we cannot understand this unless through (realistic)
idealism.

2. In the subject we have a principle of unity or wholeness,
of actual *singularity*, which is yet not the unity of an ineffable,
bare identity, but admits of variety of qualities and relations
and components. An experience has esthetic coherence which
makes it one, not barely one, but a unity-in-variety, a synthetic
unity, able to relate itself to a rich diversity. Temporally, the
subject is one through the specious present, or the quantum of
psychic becoming. Spatially, it is one through the voluminous
rather than punctiform character of its perspective, or dynamic
relationship with other entities (above all, in the human subject, with brain cells). But apart from subjects, what principle
of many-in-one is to be found? Points of space and instants of
time are surely not the answer. They presuppose units that are
actual, not mere geometrical constructs. "Electrons"? But that
is only a word for a certain class of units whose principle of
unity is not in the least furnished by the physical measurements that indicate some of the relationships in which whatever
the unit may be is known to stand. The advantage of idealism
seems patent.

3. In the subject we have a contrast of particular and universal, or of actual and potential. For every subject has purposes which contrast with actual fulfillments as universals to
their instances and as possibilities to actualities. "Ideas" are
only the more sophisticated development of this contrast. In the
alleged "non-subject" actualities, what if anything is the principle that furnishes such contrast? It cannot be desire or purpose or thought, contrasted to consummatory feeling and
sensation. What is it then? One may speak of "laws" or "principles," but these are not given in experience in the required
non-subject form. Shall the mere "matter" which is supposed to
constitute at least portions of nature be regarded, in absolutely
nominalistic fashion, as composed solely of particularities? But

not only is such extreme nominalism doubtfully tenable, but, alas, the anti-idealist is as destitute of a meaning for "particular" as he is of a meaning for universal or potential. The "chronogeometrical measurements," which are the most that an entity devoid of subjectivity can with any show of evidence be supposed to possess by way of characters, determine not particulars, but classes, geometrical types (as DeWitt Parker used to keep reminding us, thereby meeting what seems to be a real need). A shape is not a particular entity, but a generic character that such an entity (or more likely, group of entities) might exhibit. This brings us to a closely-related point.

4. A subject has *quality* of feeling or sensation. What is the principle or kind of quality in the non-subjects? The moment we become aware of any quality, our feeling acquires it as also its own quality. The feeling or sensing of blue is not the feeling or sensing of red but of blue, and differs from the feeling-of-red by all the difference (and no doubt others besides) that distinguishes the blue and red of which we are thus aware. Thus all *known* qualities are actually qualities of feeling, whatever else they may be, and all knowable qualities are potentially qualities of feeling. So the anti-idealist at best duplicates the world of subjects with a world of mere objects having no distinctive qualities whatever. Berkeley's contention is still entirely unrefuted, and to many of us is as nearly self-evident (which may not be very near) as anything in philosophy: not only are qualities when known "ideas," that is, things known, or rather felt, enjoyed, but—and this point is overlooked by most commentators—passing beyond mere verbal tautologies (as Berkeley did in the dialogue between Hylas and Philonous), it is introspective fact that qualities of color, smell, taste, thermal sensations, are qualities of feeling in the same general sense as pleasures and pains. Whitehead and many other have held the same. At least one entire book by a competent psychologist, and one by an amateur in the subject, develop the argument in detail.[3]

True, G. E. Moore might superficially seem to have refuted

---

3. F. Aveling, *The Psychological Approach to Reality,* (1929), and C. Hartshorne, *The Philosopy and Psychology of Sensation* (1934).

the notion that blue is a quality of the awareness of blue. But what Moore really shows is only that the blue cannot be *merely* a quality of the subject in the transaction, but must qualify the directly given object, whatever else it may or may not qualify. Ducasse in his disputation with Moore shows the complementary thesis, that the blue must qualify the subject, whatever else it may or may not qualify.[4] Both overlook the limitation in their evidence which calls for the addendum, "'whatever else it may qualify." With the addendum, the two positions become compatible, and the total evidence can be accounted for. Of course, the awareness-of-blue-something must feel the blue quality, and of course there is no conceivable way to feel what a quality would be like if it were simply unfelt. Anyway, awareness-of-blue is a unitary actuality of which blue is a constituent quality. But equally of course, the subject aware of blue is not aware merely of itself and its own quality, but rather, or also, of something not itself nor *merely* a quality of itself. And it will not do to suppose that the direct object is intuited as shaped yet not as colored; for the directly intuited shape *is* the outline of a color, and only as such is it intuited. It is not intuited as the outline of X, but of blue-against-red, or black-against-white. However, none of this prevents the blue or black, as quality of my feeling, from being also quality of feeling of the immediate object—nothing except the prejudice, as strong as it is little reasoned, against panpsychism, together with inattention to the fact that the direct conditions of color sense are living cells, entirely, by all established principles of comparative psychology, capable of feeling on their own. Nor is the reply cogent, if the blue-something intuited *is* cells why do we not all know the truth of the cell theory intuitively? This assumes that direct intuition is bound to be clear and distinct, and this is opposed to many facts of psychology, not to mention philosophical principles (for our intuition is not divine). We know something or some things as blue and red; but that these somethings have the further characters of cellular individuals, our visual intuitions, for all their air of simplicity and clarity, conceal from us by their lack

---

4. *See The Philosophy of G. E. Moore.* Ed. by P. A. Schilpp, 1942.

of definiteness. Neither the table we see nor the bodily cells we thereby intuit have actually the simplicity of character which vision seems to ascribe to them, or to whatever is directly intuited. If we directly intuit tables but (apart from science) "know nothing" of molecules, this is at least as paradoxical as that we directly intuit bodily process, but "know nothing" of cells. Let us play fair here. And the cells, at least, always exist, while the table might in some cases be merely a dream object.

5. In the subject there is an act of decision with regard to alternative potentialities; in the non-subjective there must be something corresponding, since the concrete is always logically arbitrary, involves something emergent with respect to antecedent conditions (this emergence being the very meaning of time or process). Now, however mysterious "self-determination" or choice or creative fiat may be in the subject, it seems totally unintelligible in the mere non-subject.[5]

6. In the subject there is intrinsic value, with the implication that to be interested in a subject is to participate in its value, share in its life, and thus enrich one's own. What then is there in the non-subject to reward interest? Its sheer non-life cannot enrich any life. And if there is nothing in the non-subject to reward interest, then the anti-idealist only pretends to think about the non-subjective; he cannot really focus his attention on it if nothing is gained thereby. Nor can the interest of the non-subjective be merely instrumental or extrinsic. For to focus on the "means" itself, as an entity in its own right, is to find a reward of attention in the entity itself as presented. One may take up study of something for extrinsic purposes; but the study itself must have its immanental values, and these must derive something from the object itself, or the lure of values will distract attention elsewhere and spoil the study. The only intelligible conception of direct derivation of value from an object is that the object has value to give, and this means, has its own values, its own life and feeling, and thus is some sort of subject. A subject's value will not, of course, wholly derive from the subjects which are its objects. There

---

5. Alois Wenzl's *Philosophie der Freiheit* (München, 1947) contains a careful, comprehensive study of the scientific and philosophical aspects of this *decision* factor.

will be an emergent plus of value; for the enjoyment of the enjoyment of another is more than the second enjoyment taken by itself. But the object must contribute something of value, or it will not determine the subject at all. For the subject as a whole is its value, and a part of the subject is a part of the value, and an independent part is an independent value. Introspection confirms all this. The more vivid is the immediate givenness of anything the more obviously does it present itself as living, and with a content of feeling in which we participate but do not create. A good example is the way sounds are given in musical experience. As Croce says, there is here no duality of mere sensations and feelings, but the whole experience is feeling through and through. Croce is mistaken only in thinking that the feeling is all merely ours. He misses the derivation of human from subhuman (cellular? molecular?) feeling. He misses, as do so many, the social structure of reality.[6]

Panpsychic or realistic idealism bases itself, not upon an "egocentric predicament," "there is no theoretical escape from the self," but upon the principle (which is no predicament), "the escape from the self, theoretical as well as practical, is into that larger community of selves or subjects the ultimate reaches of which coincide with reality." The remedy for the narrowness of experience is the sense for the vast "'ocean of feelings" (Whitehead) of which it is a part. The illusion to be overcome is not, "all reality is experience, feeling, subjectivity, value," for this is no illusion; the veritable egocentric illusion is rather, "experience, feeling, subjectivity, values, are solely or chiefly found in my self, or my kind of self." The notion of mere objects as entities which, though concrete and singular, are not in themselves subjects is the subjectivist illusion par excellence, for it is the arbitrary supposition that sub-

---

6. Besides Whitehead, Charles Peirce (*Collected Papers*, Vol. VI, Bk. 1, esp. chs. 5, 11) and Paul Häberlin (*Logik*, Kapitel 3, 6, 7; *Naturphilosophische Betrachtungen*, especially I Teil 206-209, II Teil, 110-118) seem to have most adequately dealt with this social structure. Häberlin's contributions here do not seem to depend upon his theory of "eternal perfection", which appears to me to misconceive the relations of the eternal and necessary to the temporal and contingent. (His books are published by Schweizer Spiegel Verlag, Zürich, the most recent one, the *Logik*, in 1947. The Peirce *Papers* are from the Harvard University Press.)

jectivity, that is to say, inner life, spontaneity, satisfaction and suffering, are vividly real only where vividly presented in one's own experience, and pale, negligible, or non existent where they fail thus to come into one's own possession. The limits of *our* sympathetic participation in "the life of things" (Wordsworth) is thus made the measure of reality. This might be justified in the modest form:[7] *"Perhaps* there is no subjectivity where no specific form of it is accessible to us (say, in molecules) "—were it not for this, that subjectivity is not simply a form of concrete reality, with conceivable alternatives among which, or between which and it, we might be unauthorized to choose. Our analysis has shown rather that we know nothing of a form of concreteness other than that of subjects. To say, there are individuals whose subjectivity we cannot know, and to say, there are individuals whose concrete mode of actuality we cannot know, are by all available criteria coincident assertions. Hence the alternative to panpsychic idealism is not materialism or dualism, but agnosticism or positivism. The alternative is epistemological or methodological, not ontological. Ontology, I conclude, is idealistic (in the panpsychic or realistic form) or nothing.

---

7. For a good example, see C. I. Lewis, *Mind and the World Order*. New York, 1929. P. 411.

CHAPTER FIVE

CHANCE, LOVE,
AND INCOMPATIBILITY[1]

C
HANCE, love, and incompatibility are ultimate
principles, applicable to all reality. In defending this thesis, I
wish also to discuss some of the interrelations of these three
concepts themselves. That they are interconnected is evident
on a common sense level. By chance-propinquity people come
to love each other, and there is often, if not always, some element of incompatibility between them. But of course, if the
three ideas named are to be philosophical categories, applicable
to all things, their meanings must be refined and extended
beyond the ordinary ones. Philosophy (or at any rate, metaphysics) consists in such refinement of meanings to the end
of removing their limitations. To object that in this process all
identity of meaning must disappear is to declare philosophy
an impossible enterprise. The philosopher should then cease
to encumber the academic scene. Assuming, however, that continuity of meaning is possible between the special cases drawn
from common speech and the universal conceptions arrived
at by philosophical refinement, the question is: Are chance,
love, and incompatibility favorable starting points for such
refinement?

Philosophic attempts to depreciate these ideas are not lacking. Chance has been said to be a word for our ignorance of
causes; love, to be but a form assumed by self-interest; and in-

---

1. Presidential address read (with a few omissions and differences) before
the meeting of the Western Division of the American Philosophical Association
at Columbus, Ohio, April 29, 1949.

compatibility has been held to arise solely through arbitrary negation—so that only if we declare that a possible state of affairs excludes another is it impossible, and then but verbally, that both be actualized.[2] Are these contentions justified?

Two of our ideas, chance and incompatibility, seem to be required by logic. Logic rests on the notion of mutually exclusive alternatives, P and not-P. This is a form of incompatibility. But it is also a manifestation of chance. For chance is the alternative to necessity, and if proposition P is true by necessity, then not-P is absurd and, hence, not a genuine proposition. This may indeed be the case with respect to some P's and not-P's, those affirming or denying necessary truths; but logical conceptions cannot be elucidated except on the assumption that not all truths belong to this class. Again, the logical notion of entailment, of "If . . . then," implies chance; for an "if" is correlative to an "if not," and (once more, apart from certain special cases) both must be meaningful, and thus, whichever is true, it is true by chance, not by necessity. The very notion of necessity presupposes that of chance. For the necessary is merely that which is common to a set of chances; or that of whose absence there is no chance! It is the common factor of the chances. Such a common factor is of course abstract. Assume that there are chances, and it is easy to see wherein necessity consists; assume that there is no such thing as chance, and it will, I think, prove impossible (that is, there will be no chance) to give an intelligible account of necessity. This is an example of Morris Cohen's Law of Polarity, the law that categories run in contraries so related that neither of the contrary poles has meaning or application by itself. In every set of chances, there must be abstract common factors, that is, necessities; and there seems no intelligible meaning for necessity except as common factor of a set of chances. Unconditional necessity is, of course, the highly abstract common factor of the universal set of chances, all chances whatsoever; conditional necessity is the more concrete common factor of a limited set of chances. The factor limiting the set is that *by* which, as we

---

2. See W. H. Sheldon, *America's Progressive Philosophy* (New Haven: Yale University Press, 1942), ch. iv.

say, the necessary thing is necessitated. The notion that the necessary must in all cases be necessitated by something is, however, a confusion between the restricted and the general case. The unconditionally necessary is not necessitated *by* anything, for it is merely what all possibilities or chances have in common. (Is there here a problem of logical types?) There is simply no chance of its being absent; not because anything prevents this, but because such "absence" is nonentity, denoting not even a bare possibility. (The sense in which this agrees, and the sense in which it disagrees, with the traditional notion of "necessary being" cannot here be set forth.)

Chance is non-necessity. This negative characterization, however, does not suffice. For, as just pointed out, necessity is merely an abstract aspect of a set of chances; and the concrete is more inclusive and positive than the abstract. Hence, chance must have a positive character. Peirce was one of the first to do justice to this concrete and positive character of chance.

Chance is the particularity of the particular, its Peircian firstness, freshness, spontaneity, originality—or, in Whiteheadian language, its self-creativity. Stated negatively, this is the particular's undeducibility from general concepts, which is all that distinguishes it from the general, and its undeducibility from antecedent particulars (the impossibility of deriving the total truth about it from the truth about them), which is all that distinguishes one particular state of the universe from another. If a particular were necessitated, or if all that is true of it were logically entailed, by the general, the general would be particular. For the general is the partially indefinite. Humanity in general is not the humanity of Lincoln or of Washington, but neutral to the distinction. Now to imply something definite is to be definite; for a meaning includes its implications. Hence, the general cannot imply any determinate particular coming under it. If, again, a particular must occur because another particular, called its cause occurs, then the two are logically inseparable, and indeed the later particular can only be a constituent of the earlier, and so not really later.

However, you may say, cannot a particular be implied by its cause or antecedent particular, plus a causal law? But the complex entity, cause and law, can only be either a particular or a general, and we have already seen that neither can imply the subsequent particular.

If nondeducibility is thus the very particularity of the particular, it follows that all particulars occur by chance, in our sense of the term. Are they then uncaused? Only if caused means deducible from antecedent conditions and laws. But there is another definition of cause that enables us to say that all events are caused, and that all occur by chance. Causality, on any useful definition, is whatever distinguishes from the logically possible, or the thinkable as such, that which is *really* possible in a given actual situation. Many things are thinkable that cannot here and now occur. But whatever here and now can occur is thinkable. The actually possible is thus narrower than the logically possible. There are, however, two ways of conceiving this narrowness. According to the first way, the actually possible is as narrowly limited as the actual itself. Future events that *can* occur are then just as determinate as past events that have occurred. This view is an extreme. It is also a paradox. For if real possibility is as determinate as actuality, what is the difference? Why is not the future actual already? As Whitehead says, "Definiteness is the soul of actuality." The actual particular is the fully unambiguous, that which conforms to the law of excluded middle as applied to predicates. Indeed, this law in this application is best taken as a definition of actuality. But if the future is wholly definite and thus actual, is it not present rather than future? Should we not try a less extreme and less paradoxical assumption? Why not suppose that only *past* actuality down to and including the present is fully definite (that this does not annul the difference between past and present has been shown elsewhere), and that the restricted or real possibilities which are the future so long as it is not yet present are somewhere between this fullness of definiteness and the opposite pole of unrestricted or merely logical possibility? (The more immediate future is, of course, more narrowly restricted than the more remote future, and it is but one step removed from definite actuality.) We can then say: every event is caused, that is to say, it issues out of a restricted or real potentiality; but also, every event occurs by chance, that is to say, it is more

determinate than its proximate real potentiality, and just to
that extent is unpredictable, undeducible from its causes and
causal laws. By its proximate potentiality, an event is put
into a class of then and there possible effects. Membership in
the class is compulsory for the next event, not open for its
decision. But within the class, or in so far as the proximate
potentiality is less sharply definite than actuality, there are
limits within which the event decides for itself. Insofar it
determines or creates itself; or, as Whitehead says, it is *causa
sui.* This is really less a paradox than the notion that all determination is by antecedent causes, since the latter notion merely
puts the effective determination or decision, by which possibility is restricted, back to some unimaginable beginning of
time or act outside of time. Somewhere, some*when,* somehow,
the restriction of the logically possible to the determinateness
of the actual must be effected. Where better than here and
now, in each and every event? If, however, all events thus do
the restricting, any one event can do but a certain portion of
it. The rest has already been done by antecedent events. This
antecedent, not quite complete, restriction of the logically
possible is real possibility or causality.

The classic objection to any such doctrine appeals to the
Principle of Sufficient Reason, which runs: for everything,
there must be a reason why it is as it is, and not otherwise.
This means, if anything, a denial of chance as defined above.
The Principle has an air of attractiveness. An event for whose
exact nature no antecedent reason can be given is insofar,
it seems, inexplicable, irrational; to accept it amounts to a
defeatist renunciation of the hope of explanation. However, is
explanation really thus to be equated with the possibility of
deducibility from causes or reasons? One may use the *word*
"explanation" as synonym for such deducibility; but then we
shall need another word for a broader conception of which
this is only a special case. To explain, or deal with rationally,
in this broader sense—for which a good word is "understand"
—is to spell out the relations of a thing, its wider context beyond that apparent to our sense perceptions. This context includes not only relations of similarity, repetitiveness, and
causal deducibility, but also relations of novelty, nonrepeti-

tive change, and nondeducibility. Relations of nondeducibility
are just as legitimate objects of rational grasp as those of deducibility. Indeed, as Bradley, Bosanquet, and his followers
have been making clear for us, somewhat unwittingly, the
very idea of deducibility loses its rational intelligibility the
moment we suppose that everything implies everything else.
Reason is not the mere tracing of necessary relations. It is the
correct classification of relations, with respect to necessity and
nonnecessity. A mathematician who could not see that being
square does *not* follow from being rectangular would be just
as odd as one who could not see that being rectangular *does*
follow from being square. A very famous mathematical discovery consisted in the proof that the parallel axiom of Euclid is
independent of his other axioms, does not follow from them.

If, then, to explain or understand is to classify correctly a
thing's relations, or lack of them, the statement that an event
is not wholly deducible from its antecedent causes may be as
much an explanation, as contributory to understanding, as the
statement that in part or in some features the event is deducible. We must go further. Events would become un-understand-
able, just as geometry would become so, were we to adopt the
assumption that all relations are relations of derivability.
Temporal derivability is predictability. We say that knowledge is for the sake of prediction and control. But prediction
and control, if taken without qualification, exclude one another. One predicts an eclipse, but does not control it. One
controls—from moment to moment—one's conversational utter-
ances, but just to this extent one does not predict them. To
predict is to renounce further control; to hold open for control
is to renounce prediction. If I predict what I shall say tomorrow, I imply that I shall tomorrow make no decisions concerning my speech; for the decisions must already have been
made. If Beethoven had predicted one of his symphonies, he
would have created it already; and if a psychologist had predicted it, he would have been just such a composer as Beethoven and assuredly no psychologist. The predicter of Newton
must be at least a Newton. Such absurdities may help to teach
us that—as Dewey has been contending for nearly half a century—the basic function of knowledge is not to focus a mental

camera on the future but to discover what *present* limited potentialities, that is to say, partial indeterminacies, are given for resolution in the future. The resolution itself will be the coming of the future, and to talk of predicting its form is to suppose that something can be settled while it is still unsettled. The object of knowledge is not the future as determinate, but present realities as materials from which alone the future can be made.

The ideal of absolute predictability makes sense indeed only if contemplation is in no way relative to action. The defender of chance need not go to the opposite extreme and say that contemplation is merely an adjunct to action. It suffices to say that knowing and doing have mutual relations to each other, so that neither can be solely and absolutely an end in itself. The conception of a knower who sees past, present, and future—or all time from eternity—sees them but reserves no right to make further choices with respect to them, is, I submit, a mythical one which fails to describe even what we wish knowledge to be. The myth once had a theological garb; now one finds it among logicians who have no desire to be theological. The verbal argument for the determinateness of the future, "What will be will be," is a part of this inheritance from medieval theology. It involves, as has been explained elsewhere, a doubtful conception of the relation of truth to time.[3] The future consists of what will be only in so far as its proximate potentiality is determinate; for the rest, it consists of what may-or-may-not-be. To say, "The future when it is present will have determinate character," is not by any valid logical principle equivalent to saying, "There is a determinate character which the future will have."

But can our view do justice to the role of verified predictions in testing scientific theories? In so far as science looks for causal laws, successful prediction is of course a valid criterion. To the extent that such laws obtain, and events are *not* matters of chance but determined by their antecedents in some repetitive way, prediction must be possible. A single success would not, it is true, completely establish the law, for such isolated

---

3. See *Man's Vision of God.* Pp. 99-104.

agreement with prediction might occur by chance. But repeated success without failures renders this unlikely. And in regions of nature where there is good reason to think the element of chance is small, we may proceed for practical purposes as though it were not there at all.

Of course, in addition to the aspects of absolute prediction of the future, there are the conditional predictions. If we were to set off a bomb, such-and-such would be the consequences. This is a statement about the interrelations of certain potentialities in the future, or in some unspecified time. Each potentiality has an infinite comet tail of possible or probable consequences, and whatever properties are spread throughout the tail are necessary consequences. Science enables us, then, first to set aside what definitely will happen, such as eclipses, as not suitable material for preference or decision, and second and above all, it enables us to comprehend as many as possible of the real potentialities (including those of our own character) among which we are to decide, so that we will not overlook possibilities we might wish to favor or oppose and will not imagine that such a potentiality as setting off an explosion is self-enclosed and without ramifications, other than the most obvious ones.

The hold of the Principle of Sufficient Reason upon some philosophers seems to have been due to their not distinguishing with sufficient reasonableness between various meanings of the word reason.

For what do we ask reasons? First of all, for beliefs, for theoretical decisions. The ideal of belief is that it should be determined by evidence. From this relation of belief to evidence, chance is to be excluded. The content of the belief is to represent and be necessitated by the facts. This, however, is for us only an ideal. Human beliefs are not determined solely by evidences, but in part by other factors, such as desires and wishes, whose action, so far as the ideal is concerned, involves an element of chance. In the second place, we ask reasons for practical decisions, for deliberate modes of behavior. What is their ideal? I suggest that, whereas belief has the aim of duplicating facts already in being, practical decisions have the aim of creating new facts. Science is an echo of nature, but technology is not. It is the business of an echo to be faithful. Caprice is to be excluded. But a suspension bridge is no echo, still less is a symphony or a poem. It is not even the ideal of these creations to be determined by the world in which they arise. They are to be something new, not wholly modeled on anything antecedent, including antecedent laws or ideals.

Is such creation, underivable from its antecedents, irrational? Not if words are reasonably employed. The function of reason is not, in spite of Leibniz, to dictate to the will the one best action. Reason operates with universals, and these cannot point unambiguously to a particular, hence not to a particular action. The function of reason is to point not to an action better than any other, but to a class of actions better than any other class. Ideally every member of the class is, at least for our knowledge, superior to every possibility outside the class, and equal to any within it. The enactment of any member of such a class is entirely rational, if that means immune to criticism. Suppose I say to a man, "My dear sir, you have acted unwisely; for there is another action you could have performed whose results would probably have been just as good as the one you did perform." Would he not reply, "What of it? Is there unwisdom in an action so well chosen that there is scant probability that it could have been improved upon?" Unwisdom consists in accepting a lesser value where a greater is within reach. If a man were to act like Buridan's ass and refuse, petulantly, to nourish himself because no particular food was best, would not all recognize what an ass that man was? As though a man should refuse to use a nail until he could be assured that one nail in the box was supreme! Any nail of approximately the right size is better than none, any bundle of hay better than none, and one does not starve because no food is known to be the best available. Sufficient reason in conduct is not that a particular act has a ground of preference, but that the class of acts from which a particular act is arbitrarily determined has such a ground. The ass eats hay because he is hungry, and hay is the available food; but he eats just *this* bit of hay perhaps, only because it is as *good as any* he could now have. This reason suffices for the wisest beast or man, or even, I dare affirm, the wisest superhuman being.

To the old, old query, how an act can fail to be determined by its motive, we may reply thus: An element in all motives is the desire that something new, not previously defined, should achieve definition; further, if the motive is antecedent to the act, then it cannot entirely define its subsequent fulfillment for, since definiteness is actuality, a fully defining motive would have actually all that the fulfillment could have; while, if the motive is not antecedent, then its influence upon the act belongs to the latter's self-causation and lends no support to the theory of complete determination by antecedent causes.

In the third place, one may ask for reasons for concrete events. This is the question of causality once more. The causal ideal is that events should be interesting and valuable novelties, connected with antecedent real potentiality but possessing additional determinations. One does not evaluate transactions with a friend in terms of their predictability, but in part in quite contrary terms. Only with low forms of existence, valued chiefly as means, do we tend to distinguish predictable and unpredictable as good and bad. Yet in no case is absolute predictability a valid ideal, and even if it were, events might fall short of it, as of other ideals.

An ideal still to be considered is that of freedom in the ethical sense. Most of us have read dozens of essays striving to show that ethical freedom and responsibility are compatible with causal determinism, or even that they require it. Yet I still think, with William James, that ethical freedom and metaphysical freedom are connected. All kinds of freedom have this in common, that something which, in abstraction from the entity said to be free, is undecided, by virtue of the entity acquires decision. A slave is unfree, because little is decided by him that is left undecided by others. His environment narrows down what he can do to a meager range of alternatives, out of proportion to his human capacities. Unfreedom is, then, an unduly narrow range of alternatives for decision as left open by others. Now some conclude from this that there is no unfreedom in being determined by one's antecedent character or experience, since it is still the self, though the antecedent self, which thus determines. One is not enslaved to another person. For legal purposes, perhaps this suffices. But it involves two oversights.

First, if the argument of this essay, and of many other defenses of indeterminism, is sound, to say that men are free provided they can deliberate (and act) unhampered, even though this deliberating is perhaps fully determined by antecedent factors, amounts to saying, "Men are free if they can deliberate, even though perhaps they cannot deliberate." For no real occurrence, least of all one involving the consciousness of wide alternatives and of universals, could be fully determined by its antecedents, or by any law or order which excludes chance and uncertainty. So the famous compatibility of determinism with freedom only means that the fact of ethical deliberation and its unimpeded consequences establishes freedom, regardless of what else be true or false. This is acceptable; but the question, "Could ethical deliberation occur deterministically?" is the question of compatibility over again. And the affirmative answer is assumed, not proved. Admitting that determinism cannot contradict or nullify the *fact* of freedom (nothing can nullify a fact), it remains to ascertain whether or not this fact nullifies the thesis of determinism.

Second, there is a sense, and we shall see that it is an ethically significant one, in which a human being has a different self every moment. From this point of view, to be limited by one's past self is to be limited by another, in extreme cases a very alien other at that. We return to this topic later, since the same question is involved in the attempted reduction of love to self-interest. Here I will only point out that if today's action is determined by, inferable from, yesterday's self and its environment, then by the same logic it is determined, even though in a sense mediately rather than immediately, still *completely*, by the self and world state of fifty years ago. The self of a squalling infant and its world become the repositories of the freedom that was supposedly mine. And that infant and its world were determined by the natures of the parents and their environments. (According to some forms of scientific determinism one can as well say that we determine our past as that it determines us; but this makes it but the clearer that from no point of view is there anything *otherwise unsettled* for the present self to settle, since neither past nor future leaves us any possibility of action but one.) So, as with excess of determination by neighbors in the case of the slave, so with excess of determination by antecedent character, freedom and responsibility shrink by retreating, in the one case into the environment, in the other into the past. As James said, the question of ethical meaning is not essentially one of the utility of rewards and punishments, or of praise and blame. It is a question of the locus of decision, as a real settling of the objectively unsettled. This locus cannot be in the self-identical person from birth to the present but must be in the act of the given moment. The value of human beings from which derive, for example, our rights over the lower animals, is that in us the particularization of real potentiality which is the generic nature of process occurs on a higher and more conscious level. We are important, as birds and tigers are not, because we, radically more than they, settle now what was yesterday in no sense entirely settled, and because we know that we are doing this, that we are—as Bergson says—artists of actuality, really creating new definiteness.

Quantum physics, by its category of statistical law and its principle of indeterminacy, seems to open a door to such creation. But then it appears to close it again, for practical purposes (though some authorities deny this), by implying the virtually absolute determinacy of organic action, due to the high numbers of particles involved. However, in philosophy it is categories and principles, not quantitative matters, that are at issue. If individuals on the lowest level are unpredictable, perhaps this is because they are individuals, not because they are on a low level. Now we too are individuals, units of reality, indeed we are radically more individual, and our unity is more certain, because more immediately given, than that of electrons. But we are individuals on a high level. Hence a human being need not be so predictable as the consideration of its particles alone would imply. A particle in one's brain is in the neighborhood of human thoughts and feelings, not just of other subhuman particles. Moreover, since absolute order is for all we know through physics inapplicable to units, the theory of real potentiality is at least not excluded. Assuming the theory, must there not be levels of such potentiality, as there are of units, rather than merely more or less complex cases of lowest-level potentialities? How my potentiality, or even that of an amoeba, is related to electronic potentiality may not be a matter for simple extrapolation from low-level physics, but for reasoning by analogy, tested if possible empirically. Thus, ethical freedom can, though less simply or conclusively than some perhaps have supposed, derive support from the new physics. For that physics has given up the dream, the pseudo-category, of a causality which in principle excludes chance. Of course, one may prefer to dream on.

To say that the passion for a tidy world has been a source of chaos in philosophy is scarcely a paradox. Absolute tidiness is a contradiction in terms—logical chaos. The attempt to convert men to it produces disagreement—psychological chaos. Absolute order is logical chaos, for order is a channeling of vitalities, of chance-spontaneities; and if the channeling were absolute, exact, complete—there would be no vitality, no channeling, and no order. The closer together the banks of a river, the more precisely the path of individual particles of water can be deduced from the location of the banks. But if, in the effort to restrict the particles to a precise line of flow, one were to bring the banks infinitely close together, there would be no water, no river, and no banks. This is what determinism does. In a deterministic world everything is completely determined —but this everything is precisely nothing. Whatever happens— but hold! Is not, it happens, a synonym for, it chances? The element of chance is not indeed unrestricted. There is real, not merely logical, possibility. But it is still possibility, not inevitability; it involves maybe's, not mere will-be's. Events come with a freshness, firstness, spontaneity, which is their very particularity.

There may seem to be an appearance of contradiction in what we have said so far. We have on the one hand identified chance and possibility. To say there is no chance, and to say there is no possibility, are one and the same. But we have also, it seems, identified chance with the actual particular. (The same wavering seems to be found in Peirce.) Surely possibility and actuality are not the same! Let us see if the paradox can be resolved. That a particular event occurs is never necessary, but always a "matter of chance." This means that the region of possibility with which it is correlated, or which as we say it actualizes, never implies just this determinate mode of actualization. Indeed, this determinate mode is not even one of the antecedent possibilities, but a creation out of them. A particular is not one of the antecedent possibilities or chances, but its occurrence is a matter of chance in that it was antecedently true that the real potentiality could and would be further determined in an as yet undetermined manner. The chance-character or freshness of the particular can, in truth, be viewed from two perspectives: from that of the antecedent phase of process which involves various relatively well-defined alternatives for the next phase; and from that of the particular itself which is the actualization of one of these alternatives. Here to "actualize" means more than a simple change from "merely possible" to "actual," whatever that by itself could mean, but connotes "some additional definiteness" not contained in any of the antecedently obtaining alternatives. Thus, we may agree with Bergson that it is an illusion to project an event backwards into an antecedent possibility of this very event. The antecedent possibility is as innocent of the precise quality as it is of the actuality of the event in question, and indeed the precise or particular quality *is* the actuality. But it by no means follows, in spite of Bergson (and of his predecessor Lequier, or his follower Jean Wahl) that there were no antecedent possibilities, or that there is any intellectual absurdity in the concept of antecedent possibilities. For by "possibility of particular P" we mean, if we understand ourselves, only that the previous phase of process defined itself as destined to be superseded *somehow*, within certain limits of variation, by a next phase of process. The "somehow" is not, however, a wholly undifferentiated question mark, but involves some modes of contrast, of "alternative possibilities," none of which can coincide in character with the particular which later turns up, but some one of which, or some one region of the continuum of possible quality, will later be recognizable as the *nearest* alternative or region, the one which *with the least further definition* is equivalent to the particular. This relation between particular and its possibility is only a relation of reason for the possibility, but is a real relation for the particular. Process relates itself backwards to its potencies, not forward to particular actualizations of these potencies. It does relate itself forward to the general principle, there will be further actualization, some additional definiteness or other. In this "or other" lies the aspect of chance, or possibility irreducible to any sort of necessity. So much for chance.

Incompatibility, like chance, is inherent in particularity. To be actual, concrete, particular, is to be definite, that is de-finite—limited, this but not that, or that but not this. Only pure potentiality can be unlimited, indefinite, and void of incompatibility. Real potentiality is always limited, exclusive; and actuality is the final portion of limitation or exclusiveness. A poet sitting down with an idea for a poem is in a state of mind in which many decisions as to the detail of the poem are not yet made. As they are made, more and more possibilities are excluded. Only as possibilities are thus shut out, condemned to non-actualization, can anything be actualized. The condemned possibilities are not necessarily inferior or evil. The basic incompatibility is not of good with evil, but of good with good. (Bigots, of course, fail to see this.) Moreover, there may be those who are strongly attached to some of the excluded possibilities. Every legislative act excludes things which for some are genuine values. Always someone loses or suffers. This is an element of tragedy inherent in process itself.

Ah, say some, there must be a supra-mundane, supra-temporal, immaterial realm in which the excluded possibilities may be, or are, fulfilled. This implies, in the first place, that our choices have no significance; that they settle nothing as to what is actual and what is not. If the possibilities we reject are not left unactualized, any more than those we accept, then our choices are cosmically null. In the second place, is there any meaning to the notion of an actuality which excludes no possibility? The total realm of possibility itself excludes nothing, *qua* possibility. But it excludes everything, *qua* actuality. (To explicate this fully, we should have to discuss the concept of vagueness.) An actuality which excluded nothing would be coextensive with possibility. But then what would make it actuality rather than possibility? What would be the distinc-

tion? The mere word, actuality? Is not the more intelligible
assumption that the possibilities each of us rejects are cosmically rejected, really excluded from actualization? True,
someone else can ride in the plane in my place if I give up
my seat. But the more particular possibility I give up is *my*
riding in the plane on that trip, and *this* possibility can never-
more be actualized. Every choice involves just such final and
irrevocable exclusions, valid, I suggest, for the most superior
being one can conceive. Two men who each wish to share the
central thoughts and experiences of the same woman throughout her life are striving to realize values which are incompatible
even from the most ultimate perspective. No being whatever
will enjoy both the qualities of shared experiences which can
ensue if A achieves such a place in the lady's life, and those
which can ensue if B achieves it. (To make marriage so loose
and flexible that both men can have what they want will mean
that neither can have it. Not that all reform is futile in such
matters, but that it cannot eliminate incompatibility.)

As the foregoing example suggests, logical incompatibility,
P and not-P, is merely the translation into linguistic form of
esthetic incompatibility. For, as Peirce, Bradley, and Whitehead have noted, the unity of actuality is given as a felt unity,
and its laws are laws of feeling. That one cannot feel blue and
red as characterizing the same aspect of experience is because
the esthetic values of these qualities are mutually destructive,
unless separated and made possibly complementary by some
difference of locus. The definiteness of actuality is its value,
for in the indefiniteness of mere possibility contrasts are lacking; and value is unity in contrast, beauty in the broadest
sense. The supreme example of such unity is the social harmony which is called love. Love, in the form I have chiefly in
mind, is the sense of valuable contrast and unity with another.
It is distinguished from hate or indifference as positive evaluation from negative or neutral, and from other forms of positive evaluation or liking in that its object is concrete and
singular, not abstract, general, or collective, as in love for
mathematics or for mankind. It may seem that there is a
further ground of distinction, in that the concrete object of
love may be itself a subject with its own feelings and intrinsic

values, or not such a subject. If panpsychism is correct, this distinction is verbal only. With Leibniz and many others, I hold that mere matter as such is abstract or collective, and that only panpsychism can give content to it as concrete and singular. When we love a house, we really love an abstraction, a shape, a Gestalt, or else we love a vaguely apprehended collection of singulars (molecules, say) whose characters as singulars are for us indeterminate.

However, the classic failure to see the supremacy of love is found perhaps less in the neglect or denial of panpsychism than in the age-old theory of self-interest as the root motivation. This theory has often been criticized; but few are the philosophies in which the criticism goes far enough. It is often said that if the self which is affirmed in self-interest or self-realization is the highest self, all is well. But it is not merely the kind of self which requires examination, but its numerical identity. Am I simply one self throughout my life? And is my body merely this self in its physical or spatial aspect? Then all relations of my present to my past or future are relations of identity, and likewise all relations to my body. From this standpoint, either love of others or self-love is a metaphysical monstrosity, since in the one the object loved simply transcends our identity, whereas in the other it simply remains within it. Thus, the striking empirical parallels between self-love—or self-hatred—and love or hate toward others are explained away. Metaphysically there could be nothing in common, since between sheer identity and sheer non-identity there is no possibility of mediation. Either self-love must not be called love, but just identity, or love of others cannot be love, but only a ruse of self-interest, serving the identical self, and using the other as means to this end. Again, is it much of an account of the remarkable fact that injury to certain bodily cells is felt as injury to me simply to say that I have or am those cells, or that they are my physical or material aspect? Is not the notion of absolute, substantial self-identity, as still often accepted in ethics, a logical and scientific anachronism? Since Bolzano, certainly since Whitehead and Russell, logic has known better. Psychology and physiology also know better. But the situation is confused and requires bold clarification.

The first step toward a more intelligible view is to recognize with Scholz and a number of other logicians that absolute identity of the concrete or particular is given in an event or occasion, not in a thing enduring through time, like a person or a body. The merely relative identity of the latter may be called, with Levin and Scholz, genetic identity, *Genidentität*. It is logically much weaker than the absolute identity of an event. This logical weakness is, so to speak, the ethical strength of the situation. My life consists of hundreds of thousands of selves, if by self is meant subjects with strict identity. When I love myself, this is no mere relation of identity, but an interest of a present actuality in other and past actualities, as well as in potentialities for future actualization. And these objects of my love are really loved, in that there is sympathy for them, a delight in the contrast and unity between "my" feelings, those of the present strictly identical experience, and the feelings of past or future experiences in the same sequence. It is not because there is an enduring self that there is self-love; rather, it is the relations of sympathetic memory and anticipation between successive experiences that constitute the enduring genidentical self. Memory is a form of sympathy, feeling by one experience of the feelings of other experiences. Anticipation is a more imaginative and reversed form of the same relation. It is bonds of sympathy, not between an entity and itself, but between an experience with its subject pole or focus or ego, and other experiences with their foci, that *make* self-identity.

But, am I not forgetting the body as the bearer of selfhood? In the first place, the body is many things, not just one. It is, for example, many cells, each of these many molecules. And a cell or molecule is a sequence of states or events. Each of these sequences presents the problem of genetic identity over again. Furthermore, what makes a body one's own? What binds an experience or self to a body? According to Ducasse, one's body is that with which one directly and constantly interacts. This is the minimal explication of the relation. But what is interaction? Ducasse agrees with Hume that we have no a priori insight into causal dependence, whether between physical events or between a physical and a psychical one. True, but we have such insight as between psychical events. This insight is summed up in the idea of immediate sympathy. Accordingly, but one explanation of the mind-body relation is fully intelligible. It says that every human experience immediately sympathizes with certain other experiences of a drastically subhuman type. The spatial spread of these subhuman experiences is the human body, or at least, the most intimate part of it. When I feel toothache, I suffer; am I alone with this suffering, or is it shared with others? The known fact is that I am not the only living thing involved; for nerve cells are living things. We also know that my pain occurs under conditions injurious to some of my cells. All this is as it would be if the sufferings were not mine alone, but shared with the cells.

That the entire field of esthetic experience is illuminated by the foregoing theory is manifest. The emotional expressiveness of visual and auditory data is only to be expected if these sensations are sympathetic echoes of the sufferings and enjoyments of cells. The joyous sunshine *is* joyous, not because visible light is any happier than invisible ultraviolet rays, but because cells stimulated by light are raised to a higher level of self-enjoyed activity. That sense of a world of emotions which constitutes the hearing of music is exactly what is implied if auditory experience is a synthesis of what in actuality is indeed a world of feelings, the miniature, but in its way complex and vast, world of sentient cells. The emergent over-all qualities of the synthesis lift this emotional world up to the human level, and the subhuman contributed feelings serve as signs of contrasting emotional qualities which, in generic aspect, are remotely similar between us and cells.

If the concrete sensory aspects of experience are forms of love, what about thought, or the abstract aspects? Has not logic been called the social discipline of thinking? He who will not say what he means and stand by its implications is he who will deceive his neighbors, and very likely himself, that is, he is deficient in sympathy with other experiences. Or again, take the predictive aspect of knowledge. Why predict? There is only one reason, because we sympathize with future experience. Even to know what one means by other experiences is already a social and sympathetic state.

The connection of knowledge with sympathy sets limits to the possible divorce of intelligence and goodness. Did Hitler know his social environment? He saw of it largely what he wanted to see. He saw the weakness of Chamberlain, because that fitted his desires. Did he see the strength concealed in that absurd man, the ultimate love of country and decency? Nothing of the kind. He thought Chamberlain would just go on playing the same game, and the British people with him. One whose mind is filled with the social realities, that is, the joys and sorrows and ideals of those around him, cannot maintain as an island untouched by all this his own egocentric ideal and purposes. The egoist, or if you prefer the fanatic, must manipulate or ration his sympathies (that is, his social relations). Hitler could be kind to a visiting British pacifist. Why not, since the pacifist was his unwitting ally, as well as a cripple? But Hitler could not enter too freely into certain British attitudes because there was that in them which not only was incompatible with the success of his plans but which, worse still, could only be grasped by one whose heart was not quite as Hitler's, a scene of passions that did not dare to own their own names or to see themselves from the standpoint of men of good will.

Some ethical theories seek to furnish sanction for obligation by arguing that since sympathetic emotions are largely pleasant, it is to one's interest to cultivate them. This implies that a man asking for a motive for doing good has for the time being ceased to love his fellows. But if the man has really and utterly put aside all concern for others, then almost all that is human must have left him. And insofar as he does still care about other persons, he *has* a motive for doing good to them—simply that he wants to do so. Must one have a motive for doing what one wants to do? This is to ask a motive for the motive one already has. Yet I am perpetually bedeviled with the suggestion that I must instantly cease to do good if I become convinced that my future welfare will fail to register an increment because I now act on the good will I feel. But what I need in order to act now is not a future motive, but a present one. If I presently feel concern for another and act on this concern, I do now what I now want to do, and it is absurd to ask a reward for doing what one wants to do. That I, the present self, am privileged to act out my wishes is reward enough. The account is closed. Only if I am asked to do good where I do not love or take any interest in the good of others, is it in order to raise the question of reward. For here a motive *is* needed. I may not want to do good to one I do not cherish, unless some other motive can be furnished—for instance, the hope of reward—as lure to my sympathetic interest in future experiences belonging to my sequence. Given this hope, then perhaps I can do what is asked. Frustrate the hope, and I can complain that I have been misled into a bad bargain, but only on the assumption that I did not love. Hope of reward is a substitute for the intrinsic motive of love.

Is there need for this substitute? I answer, there is political, but not ethical or religious, need. The state and society must hold out rewards, including negative ones or punishments, just to the extent that the minimal requirements of social behavior outrun the amount of love that can be presupposed in men generally. But just to the same extent, men will be legally rather than ethically correct in their conduct. They, or we—for to some extent this applies to all of us—are not really good men if, caring little for the good of others, we yet, because of rewards, promote or at least refrain from injuring that good. Bishop Paley actually presented Christian charity as simply self-regard which takes Heaven and Hell into account.[4] Berdyaev well calls such transcendentalized self-interest, "the most disgusting morality ever conceived." For it carries the denial of the primacy of love farther than an irreligious theory could plausibly carry it, since it is plain enough that in this life concern for others must often be its own reward. If, then, religion claims as its merit that it assists love by furnishing an extrinsic motive, we must reply that this is a merit only on the non-ethical, political level, the level of police action. It is, I hold, the business of the state and other social forms to provide whatever rewards or punishments the deficiencies of love make necessary and to do it so thoroughly that nothing of that sort would be left for any cosmic magistrate.

---

4. *The Principles of Moral and Political Philosophy*, Bk. II, chs. ii, iii.

The function of religion is not to enable us to act as the needs of others require without love for these others, but to enable us to love them as we otherwise could not. How can religion do this? There is only one way. We can only love or cherish people if we become aware of the beauty, actual or potential, that is in them. The religious idea in its best ethical form is that of a cosmic setting of men, and of all things, the consciousness of which exhibits them as more beautiful, more lovable than they appear when we ignore this setting. (Even the Kantian ethics, in some of its aspects, can be interpreted in this fashion.) How religion effects this enhancement of the sense for the beauty of things is a topic for another occasion. But I may perhaps mention my conviction that it can be done not by transcendentalizing self-interest, nor yet by depreciating, even from the most ultimate perspective, the concepts of chance and incompatibility, but rather by making us aware of a love which takes upon itself the totality of actualized chances, even the most painful.

Let us summarize our results and consider one or two practical applications. We have held that all happenings are to some extent by chance, and that this violates no legitimate ideal of intelligibility or reasonableness. By means of love or sympathy, what happens here and now is made relevant to what happens there and then. Human self-identity is merely a particularly important strand of this relevance. Knowledge and all interest in the past or future are forms of sympathy. Because of chance and incompatibility between possibilities, the world is partly wild and ever somewhat dangerous—as William James delighted to note. His passion here was no more than was needed to correct the bias of the great tradition in favor of some cosmic, all-detailed, infallibly executed design, some chain of syllogisms or dialectical progressions from some blessed first premise out of which, as a necessary conclusion, my hat and your toothache would eventually emerge. A chance world, that is, any world, has a tinge of tragedy in its constitution. A multiplicity of decisions irreducible to any single decision means a multiplicity of relationships that literally no one has decided, if that means chosen. Now in some of these relationships there is social harmony, in some social discord. Just which occur when is a matter of mere chance, not of choice or necessity. It follows that we must give up the dream of an existence beyond the reach of chance and tragedy. Absolute protection against conflict or suffering is a mirage.

This does not exclude every conception of providential guidance of events. Rather it means that Providence can reasonably be conceived, not as a simple alternative to chance, its mere negation or prevention, but only as a channeling of chances between banks less than infinitely close together. The function of Providence is not to enforce a maximal ratio of good to evil, but a maximal ratio of chances of good to chances of evil. That chances of evil remain is not because evil is good or useful after all, but because chances of evil overlap with chances of good. A dead man has no chance of suffering, also none of enjoyment. The principle is universal and a priori. Tone down sensitiveness and spontaneity, and one reduces the risk of suffering but also the opportunities for depth of enjoyment. All the utopias are tame, just because vitality has been sacrificed to reduce risk. Opportunity, willy-nilly, drops too. Tragedy is thus inherent in value.

For thousands of years men have sought some way to avoid recognizing this. Buddhism, Stoicism, the Christian and Mohammedan theory of Providence and of heaven as commonly interpreted, the Marxian dream of a practically conflict-free society, all are tinged with this escapism. And the result is not that tragedy is genuinely averted; just the contrary, the effect of these evasions is itslf tragic in high degree. We shall be able better to minimize tragedy when we face it resolutely as in principle inevitable, though in detail always open to amelioration. The Christian idea of the redeemed as wholly happy in the knowledge that others are damned is a tragic renunciation of sympathy which Berdyaev has gone so far as to term sadistic. The notion of an all-arranging, chance-excluding Providence is doubly tragic; it is cruel, for it compels us to try to imagine that our worst tortures are deliberately contrived for our own or someone's good by an allegedly all-loving being, and it is dangerous, for it suggests that we need not use our own resources to avert evil where possible and to help others in danger and privation.

Over and over we find practical programs vitiated by their failure to reckon sufficiently with the principles we have been discussing. Classical economics, although not so worthless or irrelevant as Marxists allege, is nevertheless weakened by two almost metaphysical deficiencies. On the one hand, it toys with the idea of an invisible hand which always and infallibly brings beneficent results out of individual motivations; and on the other, it toys with the idea that human beings should resign themselves to being, outside of family relations, simply selfish and calculating, rather than beings whose very core is love or social solidarity. Thus, it is uncomfortably close to the metaphysical blunders of trying to separate chance from tragedy and of denying the primacy of love. The market may be, and I take it it is, a marvelous mechanism for usefully coordinating actions in ways not intended by the actors; but it is not an absolute or all-sufficient mechanism. Its more or less inevitable tragedies must be carefully compared with those of available alternatives for this and that portion of our economic life. On the other hand, Marxian planning and dictatorship seem excessive limitations upon the chance-spontaneity of the many, and Marxian solidarity seems to ask both too much and too little of human love. Blanket socialistic or antisocialistic dogmas are pseudo-absolutes, not justified by the genuine absolutes, which are the ultimate factors of chance and love in correct mutual adjustment. This adjustment requires that destructive conflict arising from incompatibility of values should be mitigated without paying too high a price in loss of individuality, from which spontaneity, chance, and danger cannot be eliminated. It is through love that tragedy is, not indeed wholly prevented, but made bearable and given whatever beauty it is capable of. The love that can do this is that which expects to share with others the sufferings from which no actuality, human or superhuman—subject as all must be to chance and incompatibility—can entirely escape. Such love is not, as Plato thought, the search for the supreme beauty. In its highest human and superhuman forms it simply is that beauty.

The branch of secular science that is bringing us back to this principle, long ago, though seldom consistently, professed by religious teachers, is psychiatry. Some look to this science to finish the job of discrediting religious ideas. But, as Karl Menninger has pointed out, the basic religious idea (at least in our Judeo-Christian tradition) is identical with that of psychiatry—the idea that love is the key to life's riddles. If it be objected that religious love is *agape,* and that the love with which psychiatrists are chiefly or wholly concerned is *eros,* I reply that in this famous distinction Nygren (with whom I have discussed this matter) none too well expresses his own meaning and has often been misunderstood—as no doubt have the psychiatrists. Theologians and philosophers might well join with Menninger in longing for the day when, as he says, "We shall have accorded to love that preeminence which it deserves in our scale of values; we shall seek it and proclaim it as the highest virtue and the greatest boon. . . . Love is the medicine for the sickness of the world, a prescription often given, too rarely taken."[5] Menninger also quotes from Burton's *Anatomy of Melancholy* some words which suggest a reason why men have so often turned to lesser ideas than that of love, the reason that otherwise the greatness of their theme might have made only too plain the littleness of all that they could say about it. Burton's words are these: "To enlarge [upon] or illustrate the power and effect of love is to set a candle in the sun."[6] Behold then my candle; or rather, behold the sun!

---

5. Karl Menninger, *Love against Hate* (New York: Harcourt Brace and Company, 1942) , pp. 293-94.
6. *Ibid.,* p. 260.

CHAPTER SIX

RELATIVE, ABSOLUTE,
AND SUPERRELATIVE:
THE CONCEPT OF DEITY

IT WOULD be hard to find a philosopher who does not deal in some way, even if only by calling them meaningless, with such terms as "absolute," "perfect," "relative," "imperfect," "God," "Supreme Being." Yet it is also difficult to find a philosopher who defines these terms with the care and precision that reason requires. What would one think of a physicist who should assume that by "waves" one can only mean the longitudinal variety, and who then, from the knowledge that light does not consist of longitudinal waves, should infer that light is not *wavilinear* at all but must be classed with mere particles, "transverse waves" having been made, by definition, a contradiction in terms? Now just such fallacious reasoning from improper classification and terminology has been more the rule than the exception in both theistic and non-theistic (or positivistic) discussions of the problem of a supreme, perfect, or absolute being. Negative evidence relevant against one but not all species of absoluteness is by some thinkers taken to prove the universal sway of pure relativity; and reasons for doubting that relativity alone can explain reality are by multitudes of others taken as license for the assertion of some one arbitrarily chosen species of absoluteness. The first or relativistic form of the fallacy is found, for example, in the great Greek skeptic Carneades, in Kant (in his theory of knowledge), William James (who at times nearly escapes it), and John Dewey. The second or absolutistic form is found, so far as I know, in every im-

portant theologian and metaphysician from Aristotle to Kant
(in his theory of religion) and many others more recent, including Royce and Bradley.

The foregoing obviously assumes that there are diverse
species conforming to the generic concept, absoluteness. Of
course, if this is so, one might still refuse the term "absolute"
to all but one of the species; but this would not alter the reality
of the generic-specific structure, the lack of a terminology for
which must surely lead to fallacies. We should still need to
know what *analogous* ideas would remain to be evaluated after
we had considered the one called "absolute," or what diverse
forms of non-relativity stand as alternatives to "relativity" as
we define it— just as a physicist needs to know what alternatives
to the idea of mere particle are conceivable, and must avoid
grouping particles and transverse waves under one term in
such a way as to obscure the analogy of the two types of waves.
If there is to be argument about the reality, or even the meaningful conceivability, of an absolute or perfect being, we ought
to have before us a systematic analysis of the rationally possible
variations or analogous forms implied by the meanings, or at
least pseudo-meanings, of terms like "absolute," "relative,"
"perfect," and their contradictories. I affirm that for some two
thousand years the discussion went on in the absence of any
such analysis, and that the analysis, when made, exhibits, as
most basic, certain distinctions for which traditional terminology furnished no usable labels.

Whatever the perfect may be, it is regarded as something
better than, superior to, the non-perfect. (Of things whose value
is extrinsic or instrumental one may ask, superior for what
purpose? But suppose it is purposes or purposive beings themselves that are compared. If no purpose is ever objectively better
than another, or if, for example, a man is not on the whole
superior to an insect, then right and wrong are only pretentious
or hypocritical words for what the speaker or his group in fact
purposes. In this and other ways, it can I believe be shown
that "superior to" is not meaningless, at least for those who try
to be superior to members of subhuman groups, or to scoun-
drels.) In purely logical terms there are three possible cases of
superiority between a thing and other things, or an individual

and other individuals (it is individuals that ultimately have value). These are: superiority to *no* others, to *some* others, and to *all* others. If by "others" is meant, as shall be our usage, indifferently actualities or possibilities, then "superior to *no* others" means such that an inferior is not even possible, and "superior to *all* others" means such that a superior or even an equal is impossible (inconceivable). Thus, these cases define least and greatest being, respectively. But, as will be shown, they do not define "absolute" being, in any usual connotation. And if the greatest being (among those actual or possible) is termed "perfect," then we shall see that such perfection, or "superior-ity-to-all-others," admits of two profoundly contrasting though analogous forms.

For the truth, amazingly neglected, is that there is a cross classification no less important than the one just considered. A thing may vary, not only in its superiority toward others, but in its superiority or lack of it toward itself. A man may improve or degenerate, and thus be positively or negatively *superior to himself* as in an earlier state. It is best to term degeneration "self-inferiority," and improvement or increase in value "self-superiority," that is, to consider the relation as running from present to past rather than conversely. A thing is primarily what it is now. It is also best to consider self-superiority and self-inferiority together, as the "reflexive" case of superiority-inferiority, and the joint contradictory of these as the non-re-flexive case. For, whether change be for better or for worse, it makes a radical philosophical difference as to ultimate categories, whether there be change or not. However, we shall prove that what is superior to *all* others cannot degenerate; hence the reflexive case of this highest form of superiority will consist only of "the self-surpassing being that positively sur-passes all others, or "the self-improving being to which no other being is so much as equal." Now this concept is obviously not that of an absolute, in either of the usual senses: (1) a being wholly incapable of change, and thus "independent" of or "impassive" to the actions of other beings; or (2) a being whose value or reality is an unsurpassable limit, a sheer maxi-mum. Yet the concept does define a "best possible" being, since "other" beings are by definition declared inferior—even though the best being itself is not defined to be in its own best (or only) possible state, but rather as passing to a higher state. Thus, the notion of the "best among possible beings" has two forms, a reflexive and a non-reflexive. The latter is what is usually meant by *the* absolute; but the former, be it noted, is not what is usually meant by "relative"; so that the usual terminology presents that dangerous logical form, an inexhaustive dichotomy. The self-surpassing being that surpasses all others is, in certain respects, strictly absolute. It can be shown to be *independent* of other beings, at least for its retention of values already attained and for its assurance of surpassing other beings, actual or possible; it is also at an absolute *maximum* in this, that there can be no more universal superiority to others than superiority to *all* others. A "relativity" which includes so much of absoluteness ought not to be simply lumped together with relativity which is not thus inclusive, save as two profoundly different species of the genus; and the genus itself must be carefully construed as making this difference possible.

But not only is there a species of perfection, or superiority to all others, which is both absolute and, in another aspect, relative; there are also divisions of imperfect and least being into absolute and relative species. The non-reflexively superior to *some* others, or to *no* others, is as incapable of being significantly acted upon, altered for better or worse by other entities, as is the non-reflexively superior to *all* others. Thus *absolute-relative*, in the sense of immunity versus non immunity to influence and change, *cuts across the contrast superior-inferior*, and divides each level of superiority into an absolute and a relative form.

The reflexive and the non-reflexive, the self-increasing and the sheerly maximal, forms of all-superiority may be called relative and absolute perfection, R and A. But relative here means super-relative, a "super-eminent" type of relativity, since it involves, as we have seen, an element of absoluteness, of maximality. It might be safer to speak of "reflexive" than of relative perfection, and it is convenient that R serves equally well in either case. Also, instead of "perfection" it might be safer to use the term "transcendence" for superiority-to-all-others, since both word and phrase suggest relation to other beings, whereas the word "perfection" is dangerously loaded with the connotation, complete, therefore unincreasable, therefore without relations. Such an idea, however legitimate, is not that of superiority. Non-reflexive transcendence is what has generally been called perfection, with the unproved assumption that to be best among possible beings is necessarily to be in the best (or only) possible state of this best being.

That the absolute is the *non*-reflexively superior suggests that the merely absolute is the relative with the omission of something, and thus that relative is the more concrete, and absolute the more abstract, category. An abstraction as such obviously cannot grow or decline, but is fixed regardless of what happens. Only the concrete can be more or less, while still being itself. Self-identity in growth or decay is the mark of real individuals. Abstract qualities abstract from, omit, precisely the living process of growth from quality to quality, so that even growth as an abstraction becomes a quality that does not grow. Self-surpassing is characteristic not, as has been thought, of the imperfect versus the perfect, but of the concrete and individual versus the abstract and merely universal.[1] This was long overlooked, partly because it was believed that the inadequacy of the human mind to comprehend the divine could be mitigated only by negating our conceptions, deity being the meaning that remains after all our ideas, unworthy as they must be, are set aside. In this way change, and with it improvement, was "removed" from the idea of God. But since to omit positive aspects of experience is to abstract, how by this method can the supreme concreteness be conceived? Of course merely negative meanings, themselves abstract, must be denied of God (as perfect). He is not ignorant (though, as we shall see, he has parts or members which are, and in this way, all verified meanings, even negative, apply to God, and thus nothing in experience is abstracted from in conceiving him as R). But positive meanings, sufficiently extended, automatically

---

1. Strictly speaking, nothing can surpass itself. But in Whitehead's phrase, a "society of occasions with personal order" may be such that later occasions are superior expressions, compared to earlier, of the "defining characteristic" or selfhood of the society, and so, elliptically, the society may be said to surpass itself. The adoption, in this article, of the elliptical form does not, I think, affect the soundness of the reasoning. (See Chapter Fourteen.)

exclude negative ones, whereas negative meanings do not automatically affirm positive ones, unless we are careful to negate only negations; and if we can thus sort out the negative meanings, we can much better affirm the remaining or positive ones. In any case, relation is positive. No negating of any concept will produce the idea of relation if it is not already included in the idea negated. *Relativity is the inclusive, concrete conception;* non-relativity or non-reflexiveness (for as we have seen, these go together) is the reduction of this concrete conception to a partly negative and more abstract case.

This negative case is not a *mere* negation, such as ignorance. To "fail" to surpass-oneself-in-every-respect, or "in *some* respect to be non-self-surpassing," is the same thing as to have a self at all. For whatever self-identity is, *as* mere identity it, insofar and somehow, excludes change and self-improvement. Thus, the non-reflexive or non-relative is the necessary element of abstract identity required by the concrete, relative, or changing. On the Aristotelian principle that the concrete includes the abstract, and that the latter has no being except through this inclusion, the *relative must contain the absolute as abstract factor in itself.* Therefore, the supreme relative, the self-surpassing-and-all-other-surpassing, contains the non-reflexive or absolute in its supreme, that is, all-other-surpassing, form.

In relation to others, the important distinction is between superior and non-superior. For, though non-superior means the disjunction, inferior or equal, this duality is of secondary importance. If an entity is superior to *no* others, it is at the bottom of the scale of beings whether it has equals there or not; and if it is superior to *some* but not all others, it is in the middle of the scale, since it is demonstrable that there cannot be a plurality of equals at the top of the scale, and thus "not superior to all" is the same as "inferior to some." Accordingly, we set up our scale in terms of superiority and its denial. (We could also use inferiority and its denial, but the lessons would be the same.) It is further to be noted that, as we shall show, the being which is superior to *all* others cannot be self-inferior. We therefore construct our table of grades of being as follows. (By "others" is meant beings, *whether actual or possible,* not individually identical with the being in question.)

THE GRADES OF BEING FORMALLY ANALYZED

I. Lowest Grade: Superiority to *No* Others, *Least* Being.
   i infinitesimal: the *reflexive,* self-unequal, dynamic form.
   The relative or concrete minimum (*e.g.,* a consciousness
   closer than any assigned distance to unconsciousness; or
   the scale of beings as approaching, or advancing from,
   nonentity as lower limit).
   n null: the *non-reflexive* or static form.
   The absolute or abstract minimum. Nonentity.

II. Middling Grade: Superiority to *Some* Others, Ordinary or
   Imperfect Being.
   r relative: the *reflexive* form.
   Ordinary concretes (*e.g.,* a man).
   a absolute: the *non-reflexive* form.
   Ordinary abstractions (*e.g.,* honesty).

III. Highest Grade: Superiority to *All* Others, Transcendent or
   Perfect Being.
   R Relative (in eminent sense; superrelative) : the *reflexive*
   form.
   The concrete maximum; the self-surpassing surpasser of
   all. (God as self-contrasting life, process, or personality.)
   A Absolute (in eminent sense) : the *non-reflexive* form.
   The abstract maximum; the self-unsurpassing surpasser
   of all others. (God as mere self-identical essence abstracted from the fullness of his accidents, the contingent
   contents of his awareness.)

This analysis conforms to the current demand that philosophy make use of logical structures, in the strict sense in which
these are capable of mathematical expression. The six forms of
being follow mathematically from the purely formal properties
of "superior to" as obtaining between a thing and all, some,
or no other things, and the formal properties of self-inequality
as obtaining or not obtaining between a thing and itself in an
earlier state. In both cases we have a formally exhaustive
division. We assume initially only such matters of common
life, comparatively neutral to schools of philosophy and theology, as that there are degrees of value attaching to individuals
and their states, in comparison with other individuals, or with
earlier states of the same individuals. How else can we have

rational philosophical discussion save on such a neutral basis, surveyed for its formal possibilities, which are then, and only then, to be evaluated competitively in the light of such evidence as we can find? The usual procedure has been to put the supposed evidence on the most difficult points into the very terminology by which the alleged search for evidence is from the first conducted! And in this regard theists and skeptics have often been very much alike.

It will be seen that the chief novelty of the table is the division of each of the three grades of being into two radically different forms. (I must in this chapter pass over the problems of interpretation presented by the forms of least being, *i* and *n*.) Traditional arguments proceed as though there were no such paired structure. They treat self-superiority as though it were an imperfection in the same sense as is non-superiority to others; and this is a monstrous assumption which settles by definition the answers to basic philosophical issues. To be less than another, to fail to have something good possessed by another, is to be less than reality as a whole inclusive of self and other. Thus, it is definitely not to be the supreme being, which must then be reality as a whole. But to fail to possess actually all the value the being *might itself possess* is not necessarily to be less than reality as a whole, and not necessarily to be inferior to any actual or possible "other" being, but only perhaps to a possible state of the same being. For suppose this being is possessed of power to appropriate completely all actual being and value when, and as, actualized. Then, any possible *other* being could become actual only by constituting, with its entire value, a part of the value of the all-appropriating being, which therefore must in any possible situation remain supreme.

The sole sense in which the possibility of self-increase implies defect is this: the being would not already possess as actual "all possible values." But this sense of "defect" is really nonsense, for all possible value as actual is doubly absurd, since it makes possibility and actuality completely co-extensive and for all purposes identical (why do we try to actualize possibilities if in the Supreme Being they eternally are actual, whatever we do?), and since it implies that mutually incompatible possibilities are co-actualized. Professor Sheldon has

attempted, indeed, to show that possibilities are incompatible
only conditionally, or upon certain assumptions. Incompatibility is, he says, tautological.[2] I should say it is tautological,
at least in this sense, that to "actualize" *means* to do *this* and,
for that very reason, *not* to do *that*. Actualization *is* determination of the indeterminate determinable, limitation of limitless
potentiality. This "condition" is not arbitrary, for without it
no distinction between actual and possible could be conceived
and both terms would vanish in meaninglessness. The universe
can contain me doing what I at this moment do, and it could
have contained me doing something else which I might have
done at this moment. The universe cannot contain me doing
both things. (Nothing I might do later would be quite the
same as any of the things I could do now. No *infima species* of
possibility ever recurs.) Nor can the universe contain me doing
the one thing and a different individual doing the other. To
substitute "God" for universe changes nothing, since the
essential difficulty is that my choices are meaningless if, whatever I choose, the possibilities not chosen can be actual in some
other being. Individuality is meaningless and valueless if the
very individual value that my personality makes possible, but
which I leave unactual, is possible for some other personality.
All our concepts collapse if one takes this path.

If there is a heavy burden of proof in philosophy, it is upon
the view that a being which is everything possible, that is,
nothing determinate, unutterable confusion, is a possible or
actual being. Only after attempting to formulate the conception of highest possible or perfect being in some less dubious
way should one draw the positivistic conclusion that perfection
is nonsense, or the obscurantist (but traditional) conclusion
that perfection defined nonsensically is nevertheless real.

In interpreting *R*, I have so far taken it for granted that a
self-contrasting being surpassing all others will contrast with
itself only through increase, never decrease, of value. This is
to be justified as follows: if absolute immunity to degeneration
is possible in a self-contrasting being, then such immunity,
being an excellence, must be possessed by the self-contrasting

---

2. W. H. Sheldon, *America's Progressive Philosophy.*

being which is superior to all possible others. But is the immunity possible? Does not mutability imply corruptibility? On the contrary, there are good reasons for asserting that there can and even must be a mutability which is exclusive of decay. If destruction is on as ultimate a level as creation, then creation must in principle be more or less futile. Unless creation is at least dominant, it is absurd, accomplishes nothing. But more than this, can there really be ultimate destruction at all? The very strangeness of the word "unbecoming" (in the here relevant sense) suggests that the becoming of experiences (and it is these which have value) is not in principle nullified by any contrary process. Events "come into" being, but do they really pass "out of" it? "The Moving Finger writes . . . nor all thy Piety nor Wit shall lure it back to cancel half a Line." What-has-occurred forevermore will have occurred, and as "having occurred" continues, with all its qualities (hence, its values?) to enjoy a place in reality.[3] On the other hand, the future need not consist of definite "will-be's" which from all past time, have been in being as things which "were to be."[4] Such a preformed or static future has been widely disputed ever since the Greek logicians, and never so widely as today. But the post-formed (or still and henceforth formed) past seems unavoidable. Events as past still have been all that they have been, that is that they ever were, except that now they are such with the *additional* status or relation of "having been" it. Otherwise, there could be no determinate truth about past events. For truth is agreement with reality, in some cases with a real has-been.

The upshot is that reality as a whole of real events, together with whatever there may be besides events, is a growing whole. It surpasses all other beings; for all are parts of it in being and value. It acquires new members but loses none. It increases but does not decrease; it is mutable but incorruptible. Or it is mutable only so far as addition is mutation. It appears that it

---

3. That this does not contradict its pastness I have shown in my *Man's Vision of God and the Logic of Theism* (Willett Clark & Co., Chicago, 1941) pp. 129 ff., 286 f.

4. Some aspects of the future are may-or-may-not-be's, and propositions asserting them either as will-be's or as will-not-be's are *all false*. (*Op. cit.*, pp. 98 ff.)

is or involves *R*, reflexive transcendence, as we have interpreted this. And reality as a whole cannot be impossible. (To conceive it is not to violate the theory of types, or to adduce a concept without contrasting concepts; for the whole contrasts with its parts, and in its actual state or members contrasts with its possible ones; while there is no need to suppose it to involve the "class of all classes." The whole in its actuality includes all that is actual, and in its potency all possibility; but the sense in which classes are actual, or potential, or capable or incapable of forming a totality, is a matter for special inquiry.)

At this point many will be saying that the whole of reality is too amorphous or lacking in integrity to be regarded as perfect, or as superior to any other even possible being. To this contention I reply that the non-integrity of the reality inclusive of all others is at least not self-evident. Again, it will be said that the inclusive reality must be completely responsible for the actions, however sinful or unwise, of the included realities or members, that human freedom must be denied, that the whole-being must believe the beliefs of the members, however false, that it must be "imperfect" in the same sense as the members, or that it must be "impersonal." However, these are all bits of loose thinking left over from pre-analytic discussions of this subject. They fail to see the quite essential distinction between "God is all things" and "God includes all things," or between pantheism and panentheism. These concepts can be very exactly defined, and when this is done it will be plain that refutations of pantheism have no power to invalidate panentheism or establish its traditional alternative of a supreme being which is non-inclusive of lesser beings.[5]

As we have seen, what does not grow can be an abstract element in what does grow. A man may take on new qualities, but these qualities do not take on new qualities. There is then no need to choose between the reality of fixed qualities and the reality of growing things. Similarly there may be no need to choose between *A* and *R*, or *a* and *r*. They may both be real (though both cannot be equally concrete) and real in the same

---

5. See my articles on Pantheism, Panentheism, God as Personal, Omnipotence, Transcendence, in Ferm's *Encyclopedia of Religion*.

being. A being which in *all* aspects surpassed all beings not itself, but in *some* and only some aspects surpassed also itself, would in the self-surpassing aspects be *R*, but in the remaining aspects *A*. It would have a fixed abstract character, but, like an at all times equally honest man exercising his honesty in diverse circumstances, it would nevertheless experience new content.

Possibilities being inexhaustible (not all being compossible), *perfection can be "absolute," non-reflexive, or a sheer maximum, only in those dimensions of value which are neutral to the distinction between actual and possible.* Now some ways of measuring value which are proper in theology have the required neutrality; for they refer to a *type of relation* (between a being and other actual or possible beings) that can be at its best regardless of how many or which possible other beings are actual. This type of relation may be called "adequacy." Thus, knowledge may "correspond" adequately to its objects, regardless of which of these objects are actual and which only potential, provided the actual ones are known as actual and the potential as potential. And the will may respond rightly, or with ethical adequacy, to a world, regardless of just what possible things are actualized in the world. So omniscience and perfect righteousness are not sheerly maximal concrete totalities, but are sheerly maximal *types of response* to the *de facto* concrete totality (which is never the greatest possible). They are the best possible modes of response to whatever is responded to. But the total value enjoyed through this response, the satisfaction, the loving joy, must depend also upon the particular things, the concrete totality, responded to; and, since this totality cannot reach an absolute maximum, neither can the total value. "All possible beautiful and satisfying objects, all known as actual" is nonsense. And if one holds that possible objects could be just as satisfying if left unactualized, one is implying that actualization is superfluous; which is little worth discussing with one who goes on living, that is, actualizing. Take it how you will, no maximum beyond increase can be formulated for that concrete value of experience which we call happiness. The consequence is that either the perfect being is without happiness or concrete value in any intelligible sense (and then it is anything but perfect), or it is superrelatively, reflexively, not just self-equally, superior to others, *R*, while yet in relational adequacy of knowledge and activity to these others it is, in its superiority, absolute and immutable, or *A*.

In this way we escape the age-old error of identifying the absolute or sheerly maximal with the greatest or most real. The purely absolute cannot include relative realities, for if it did it would be relative; similarly, the purely necessary and fixed cannot include the contingent and growing. (Nor is anything gained by calling the relative or contingent unreal, or real in varying degrees. For it would still be untenable that all possible degrees and forms of relative unreality are contained in the absolute, and the latter's pure absoluteness and necessity would be as much contaminated by relative unreality as by any other relativity.[6]) *Relativity cannot be put inside the absolute as such; it must be outside it, if there is an absolute; but then there is also a third something which is more than either, a whole of reality, with an absolute factor and relative factors. This whole is reflexively transcendent, self-surpassingly superior to all, R, yet with an abstract element of non-reflexive transcendence or absoluteness, A.* The whole-being in its concreteness has the value which absolute adequacy can derive from the given parts, hence, the utmost value they are capable of yielding, and more than is or could be enjoyed by any other being, but still not absolute value, for "absolute parts," or "absolute richness of value accruing from relative parts," is meaningless.

Thus, the one and the many are reconciled, at the same time that the idea of perfection is given intelligible meaning. *What is purely absolute cannot be relative, even in any part or factor of itself. But what is super-relative (reflexively transcendent) can be absolute in one aspect or abstract element of its being, and can also contain a world of relative things as its* concrete parts. The parts determine, in interaction with the radically superior determining power of the whole-being, the

---

6. Illusionistic monists (Sankara, Bradley, most recently B. Blanshard in his *Nature of Thought*) seem to have overlooked the concept of *R* Transcendence, and thus to have argued from an inexhaustive dichotomy. Also, Bradley and Hegel tell us that it is the abstract that is relatively unreal, whereas we have shown that the absolute is abstract and only super-relativity is wholly concrete.

accidental *de facto* state of that being (the contingent content of its experience). Without any one such part or set of parts, the whole-being would still have been itself, but itself in a somewhat different state of experience and value, and with some alternative part or parts.

Reflexive perfection is the only all-inclusive conception, the only one which describes, in outline, the full context of its meaning. It explains not only parts but the whole, not only being as opposed to becoming, but the being of the already become, which "lives forevermore" (Whitehead) or incorruptibly. It can even explain the truth that there is evil as well as good. For while the superior to all must will only the good, evils can nevertheless result from the volitions of the member beings, according to the great principle of Fechner's psychology, which is fully in accord with our definition of R.[7]

The inclusive or whole-being enacts or suffers all activity; it does not enact all or suffer all. Its absolute perfection of power over the parts is an absoluteness of adequacy to the parts and their needs, especially their need, which is essential to their reality, of making their own decisions and hence, possibly, their own mistakes. The whole is "all possible value" only in the sense that the possibility of any value is identical with the capacity of the inclusive being to possess it, through the required members and the required action and passion. However, as R the whole is all *actual* value, for it enjoys all enjoyment that occurs anywhere. It suffers all the suffering also; and indeed a given enjoyment cannot be abstracted from the sufferings which, in some degree, are always entwined with it. The reflexively perfect God is a suffering God, who endures all evil, though he does not enact it or become evil in the active sense of wickedness. A suffering God has for nearly twenty centuries been symbolized by the cross, while during nearly the same period philosophy has not known how to grasp the idea in technical terms. Massive prejudice neutralized Fechner's great chapter on "God and the World" in the *Zend-Avesta*. Schelling's later writings (c. 1811-12: see *The Ages of the World*, transl. by Bolman, 1942), which had a somewhat simi-

---

7. *Man's Vision of God*, pp. 291 ff.; Fechner, *Zend-Avesta*, Ch. xi.

lar import, were abstruse and were neglected. But more recently, the passivity of God has been asserted more clearly and
much more frequently. I cannot but hope the change is permanent.

In sum, there are three grades of being, purely inferior,
purely superior, and mixed or inferior-superior. Each grade
has two forms, a reflexive, self-contrasting form, which is concrete and relative; and a non-reflexive or self-equal, abstract
and absolute form. The absolute form is the element of mere
being, the relative form includes, besides mere abstract being,
the concrete being-of-becoming, and this involves both the
becoming and the having-become of concrete events, *i.e.*, process. There is just as much a supreme form of process as of
mere being; moreover, the process includes the being as the
concrete includes the abstract. The attempt to make the absolute as such the most real or inclusive entity inverts the relations
of abstract and concrete, committing the fallacy of misplaced
concreteness. The self-contrasting may and must have an aspect
of self-equality; but the merely self-equal all by itself is nothing,
an abstraction or quality abstracted from everything, qualify-
ing nothing.

The traditional arguments for the existence of God were
contaminated—and traditional criticisms of these arguments
rendered in so far irrelevant to the question whether God exists
—by the confusions or absurdities in the definitions of God
which they were designed to support. There have been arguments to prove or disprove a purely absolute being; and others
which, if they proved anything, could only establish the existence or non existence of a purely relative and contingent God;
but what is hard to find (until Schelling or later impossible) is
an argument explicitly and clearly bearing on the question
whether there is a God both absolute or necessary and (in another aspect) relative or contingent, that is, reflexively transcendent. Such arguments are possible,[8] and only when philosophers

---

8. Plato, in the *Timaeus* and the tenth book of the *Laws* might have been, but
was not, interpreted as pointing to such an argument. See R. Demos, *The Philosophy of Plato*, Ch. v. Among recent thinkers whose idea of God agrees best with
the *AR* concept are: Varisco (*Know Thyself*, 1915, p. 323); Whitehead [see the
great last chapter of *Process and Reality*; also my "Whitehead's Idea of God" in

have considered them with something of the care they have bestowed upon arguments dealing with a less intelligible conception will it be time to say that the arguments for God's existence have been either validated or invalidated. The question we need to investigate concerns the existence of a being whose nature conforms to the formal structure of the idea: "surpassing self and all others."

The Philosophy of Alfred North Whitehead (ed. by P. A. Schilpp, 1941)]; W. P. Montague (*The Ways of Things*, 1940, Ch. vi and Part II, sec. vi) ; and D. H. Parker (*Experience and Substance*, 1941, Ch. xvi) . There is also E. S. Brightman (*The Problem of God*, 1930, and *A Philosophy of Religion*, 1940, Chs. v, ix, x) : Brightman neglects the distinction between pantheism and panentheism, and does not accept or perhaps understand the James-Fechner-Whitehead principle of the compounding of experiences (see James, *Pluralistic Universe*, Chs. vii, viii) . However, the reasons for conceiving God as receptive and temporal have seldom been so forcefully stated as by this writer.

PART II: RELIGIOUS VALUES

CHAPTER SEVEN

THEOLOGICAL VALUES
IN CURRENT METAPHYSICS

T HE title of this chapter applies also to much of the content of previous chapters. The present essay is, in fact, a restatement of many of the main points already affirmed. It is hoped, however, that some fresh light will be thrown upon the basic position.

Whitehead used to remark that there must probably have been some stage in the development of medicine prior to which it was safer to rely upon common sense than to call in a doctor. Now, said he, the question is: Has metaphysics yet reached the point where its doctrines give better guidance than the reflections of men untrained in the subject? So long as metaphysicians disagree to the extent that they now do, an affirmative answer to Whitehead's question will be troublesome to defend. And if metaphysics is unable even to surpass common sense, why should religion, which claims insights on a level of uncommon sense, of revelation, look to metaphysicians for enlightenment?

However, this at least seems plain: whether or not theological doctrines *ought* to develop in independence of metaphysics, they have not generally done so in the past. If theology is to be emancipated from metaphysical assumption and argument, this result will have to be achieved in the future; it cannot be taken over ready-made from the work of older theologians, whose writings contain many a bit of secular metaphysics and often what some of us must regard as particularly bad metaphysics. Even Barth, I suspect, is not really free from this defect.

Metaphysics may be defined as the "rational and secular study of the universal traits of experience and existence." For example, if suffering and change are held to be universal, this is a metaphysical tenet, which is illustrated by the doctrine of a suffering and changing God but contradicted by that of an impassive and immutable one. By definition, there can be no exception to a metaphysical principle. A "secular" study is one which assumes no evidence other than such as is accessible to any intelligent man who *sufficiently* reflects upon our common human experience. Special religious gifts or experiences are not to be taken in evidence. They may be used to suggest hypotheses, but any *decision* as to true or false is to rest upon more generally accessible phenomena. Religious data are not excluded, provided they are common property, that is, capable of detection, in some degree, in the experience even of (sufficiently observant) atheists.

It is not an assumption of metaphysics that all truth can be known by the secular method but only that whatever *can* be known by that method, that is, from common experience, is worth knowing in that way. If, in addition, some persons can know certain things by uncommon experiences, so much the better. If theology claims to answer (for certain groups of people) some of the questions which metaphysics leaves open, the metaphysician will not reject this claim a priori; though he will, of course, say that the answer is at most established for those people, not for mankind. But suppose metaphysics and theology give incompatible answers to the same questions? Which is to give way? I answer, "Neither." Not that what is true for revelation may be false for (secular) reason but that both secular reason and revelation are fallible. Revelation is uncommon religious insight, divinely granted it may be, but (in spite of the claims of the Roman church and other "fundamentalists") humanly received and expressed and therefore fallible—possibly, and even probably, distorted either by sin or by stupidity. And secular human reasoning likewise cannot be performed in such a way as to make mistakes impossible. Hence in case of conflict between theological pronouncements and metaphysical conclusions, no man is entitled to feel altogether sure which is in error; though at least one of them must be so. Any metaphysician or any number of metaphysicians may have made a mistake; but, on the other hand, even though the philosopher be an atheist, he cannot be certain of his atheism and cannot be certain that the vision of God which theology codifies is not, after all, an experience of reality more profound or adequate than any nonreligious experience. Thus, wherever metaphysics and theology are out of harmony, it seems that each discipline ought to stand by its position pending further light by its own method; yet the fact that the other discipline reaches a contradictory result should be taken on *each* side as secondary evidence (additional to the general fallibility of the human mind) of the need for caution and for renewed effort to discover flaws in its own position.

The difficulty in applying this principle is, of course, that there are many schools of theology and also many of metaphysics. But any tendency toward convergence on either side should give pause to those of the other who are out of harmony with the convergence. I say, "should give pause," not "should put to confusion or flight." For the majority may be wrong in any science or in any religion.

Is there any convergence in metaphysics today? I think that there is not enough convergence to furnish a very cogent argument, but enough to be worth considering. I take it that Bergson, James, Fechner, Alexander, Whitehead, Varisco, Scheler, Ward, Boutroux, Montague, Parker, Garnett, Hocking, Boodin, and others, including the present writer, are in a certain rough agreement that is somewhat more striking and representative of metaphysics since about 1850 than is any other trend. True, Santayana was rather outside the group, as was Husserl; while Dewey was half in and half out of it, Russell is mostly outside, and the Logical Positivists reject metaphysics altogether—supported in this, though not completely, by C. I. Lewis. But these men have failed to familiarize themselves with the metaphysical developments referred to, and hence their failure to adopt them may rest chiefly upon lack of knowledge.

Suppose, for the moment, there is some such partial convergence as I have indicated—though so far only by citing names. Of what significance can this be for theology? You might argue that Christians are an élite minority, that a secular study, drawing on average human insights, will inevitably reflect the non-Christian or even anti-Christian bias and character of ordinary men. You may even argue that to respect these average insights—or seeming insights—is to allow original sin to establish itself in our very doctrines. I reply, first of all, that original sin is not wholly escaped even by theologians—and sometimes I think that they are especially subject to it, particularly in their theoretical work, where pride of opinion and other temptations assail them.[1] I reply, secondly, that in so far as metaphysicians are honest and competent in the application of their own method, they will decide issues only where they have positive warrant for a decision and will not adopt doctrines on a mere basis of feeling or preference, such as a distaste for Christianity or a disinclination to recognize God. They may have to struggle hard to avoid yielding to these tendencies and may not wholly, or nearly wholly, succeed; but just so far will they fail as secular metaphysicians, for it is the professed ideal of their method to avoid nonrational procedures. If, then, they achieve any success at all, their results will have *some* validity, Christianity or no Christianity, sin or no sin. And, finally, the direction which their thought has taken harmonizes rather well with certain developments in recent theology.

What, then, is the content of the convergence of which I have been speaking?

The simplest summary of the doctrine is that it is a *social theory of reality*. By "social" is not meant "human," though, since human beings do form societies, there will, according to the theory, be an analogy between any reality whatever and a human being; just as, for "mechanism," there is an analogy between an automobile and any other natural system. But the analogy need not in either case be close or specific; thus, the social theory rests upon the utmost generalization of the resemblance between various types of social beings, of which man is but one. The theory (See Chapters One and Three) holds that the insentient, dead, and mechanical is secondary to, or even

---

1. Niebuhr has pointed out that philosophers are to some extent less exposed to the sin of pride than theologians (see Reinhold Niebuhr, *Human Destiny*, p. 230).

a mere appearance or special case of, the sentient, living, and social. A machine is to be interpreted as a low-grade society, one whose members are on a low level of feeling and creative action, a society in which uniformity and routine almost completely overshadow, though they do not eliminate, individual variations and freedom. A machine is thus a society that does about what it can be expected to do, or is made to do, whereas a high-grade society is always full of surprises and eccentricities.

There are two chief types of societies: those in which *all* the members are of similar grade and those in which there is one radically superior and, by its superiority, predominating member. The living human body is a society of cells (relatively low-grade individuals) plus one high-grade individual, the human personality whose body it is. What we call animate matter, as Leibniz was the first to suggest, differs from the inanimate precisely in that in the latter there is no dominating member of the society. A pile of sand is an obvious example. No one thinks there is a "soul" of the pile, simply because the pile does not act in a sufficiently organized, unitary way to suggest that it embodies any purposes inhering in the pile as a whole. But when we come to individual molecules, atoms, or electrons, the lack of dynamic integrity characteristic of many larger objects can no longer be so confidently asserted. The "inorganic," as a clearly verifiable fact, is a mass phenomenon. Every individual thing above the electronic level is really a society of things, or a society of societies, etc. Some of these societies are without any super-member capable of integrating their activities sufficiently to constitute them besouled organic bodies. Others possess such a member.

The remarkable fact is that this theory, however speculative or fanciful it may seem to some, can be so formulated or modulated as to fit not only any facts now known to science but any fact which could conceivably be known. That there might be high-grade societies, like human groups, is obvious, given the theory above outlined. On the other hand, it is equally in order that there may be societies so low-grade in their members, and so lacking in a dominating, organizing super-member, as to present the appearance, to beings limited as we are in knowledge, of mere dead machines or inert masses.

The social theory of existence denies that any individual unit of reality (excluding mere composites from the class of "unit") is absolutely without feeling or free creative action. Thus, it is the precise contradictory of materialism and of determinism—even if these doctrines are asserted of but a portion of nature. It is the contradictory of these doctrines, but not their contrary or extreme opposite; for it admits that some individuals have the barest or most trivial sentience and creativity, so that the idea of mere unfeeling "matter" behaving with monotonous regularity is only the ideal negative limit to which actuality can in fact more or less closely approximate.

Our theory denies also that any individual is totally without sensitivity or responsiveness to other individuals, that any existent is what it is without regard to what other individuals are. This is the denial both of absolute monism, the assertion that there is but one real individual, and of absolute atomism —defining an atom as "an individual which does not in its own being involve relationship and relativity to other beings."

God, if defined as *wholly* self-sufficient, absolute, and independent, would be precisely such an absolute atom and consequently is excluded by the social theory. Not that this theory is wholly "relativistic," but it must regard any absoluteness of God as *only one aspect* of his being, which in another aspect must be relative to all other beings, and in this sense, as in other senses, supremely social. A social being receives from others as well as gives to them. It takes upon itself their joys and sufferings, and in this way it is enriched, though also troubled, by their lives. It cannot in every sense and aspect be "independent" of them or incapable of receiving from them additions to its own being, however "complete" in some aspects is this being.

The social theory is temporalistic, the denial of any notion of a purely timeless or immutable existent. Sociality is a relation of streams of experiences,[2] an action and reaction between living beings whose life consists as truly in changes as in endur-

---

2. "Stream" is not obviously a social image; but Whitehead has shown how personality can be analyzed into a succession of experiences connected by social relations (one sympathizes with past and future states of "one's self"). See especially *Adventures of Ideas*, pp. 258 ff.

ance or self-identity. Not that "everything" changes but that every existent, individual, such as a man, or God, involves change. This is compatible with and even implies that individuals have abstract aspects which are changeless. A changing whole may have some unchanging factors, since the change of any factor suffices to change the whole. And a changing individual must have some unchanging factor, since the change of all factors and properties would abolish the individual. So a social equivalent for the immutability of God is possible, provided it be admitted that he is not in every aspect immutable.

The social theory, then, is pan-psychistic, pan-indeterministic (or pan-creationistic), pan-relativistic, and pan-temporalistic, in the sense that every concrete being has psychic, free or creative, relative, and temporal aspects. The holders of the theory seem to agree in accepting the existence of God. How, indeed, could a world society of free individuals exist and endure, and even to a minimal extent avoid chaotic, mutually destructive conflict, except thanks to a supreme member able to dominate the rest by its influence and thus coordinate their activities into a world order, a single complex society? God, in this doctrine, is the supreme *socius*, the all-dominating member of the cosmic society, the ideally and universally social being, as contrasted to beings locally and defectively social. God is held to love all, not just a few; always, not just at times; in all their being, not with neglect of this or that aspect; and his influence in the universal society will be paramount and the basis of its integrity.

The older metaphysicians and theologians, the latter surely under influence from the former, assumed a partly unsocial conception of reality in general and of God in particular. They excluded the lowest and the highest levels of being from the sphere of the social. "Inanimate" nature was thought too inferior, and God too superior or perfect, for the union of dependence, mutability, and feeling involved in sociality. The new doctrine makes perfection, by definition, the highest instance of reality as social, since to be real and to enter into social relations are for this doctrine inseparable. Thus, God really *is* love, without cavil or inconsistency. In whatever sense a social being can be absolute and independent, God may be absolute and independent—but in that sense only; and in whatever sense a social being must, in principle and therefore even in the ideal case, depend upon others, God is in *that* sense dependent and relative. Also, even the least of beings, say an electron, will in no respect totally lack sociality—however trifling and ultra-simple its social life, that is, its life of sympathetically responsive and at the same time creative feeling.

It is demonstrable that the pan-relativism inherent in the social theory does not exclude a being absolute or independent in *some* aspect; though it certainly excludes a being absolute in all aspects. The social is a synthesis of dependence and independence, as it is of change and permanence, or the one and the many, or order and creative freedom, or quantity and quality. It is the only conception of the universe that plays no favorites among the categories but assigns to each a place in reality as such. It treats law and freedom, unity and variety, activity and passivity, as equally real and ultimate, each having its function in relation to the other. In this balance as to the categorical claims lies the superior rational coherence of the social theory. Where other theories explain away one or more of the universal traits of actual or conceivable experience, the social theory explains them all by their mutual relevance to each other.

To be social is to weave one's own life out of strands taken from the lives of others and to furnish one's own life as a strand to be woven into their lives. It is giving and receiving, neither having priority over the other. ("It is more blessed to give than to receive" refers to a special kind of giving, where the gift is of that material kind—consisting in low-grade societies—whose use by one interferes with its use by another.) A strange prejudice governed both philosophy and theology for two thousand years. This was the supposition that, to conceive the highest being, we must maximize in conception the aspect of giving, but minimize that of receiving, maximize activity but minimize passivity, maximize unity but minimize variety, maximize permanence but minimize achievement of the new. This prejudice controlled the thinking even of atheists; for the God they rejected—as though no other could be in question—was a God so conceived. One has only to look squarely at this way of conceiving God to see that it is without rational basis. Giving and receiving are by no requirement of coherence related as mere contradictories, like knowledge and ignorance, so that, where the first is greater, the second must be less. It is just as true that a man is passive in many ways in which an atom is not as that he is active in many ways in which an atom is not; and the superiority of the man is precisely as clear in the one case as in the other. Read poetry to the man, and he may be molded and modified by this influence in manifold and subtle fashion, but read poetry to the atom, and any "effects" upon it will by comparison be slight and narrowly limited in range. A man can sympathize with any living thing he sees suffering or enjoying, or imagines to do so, and this sympathy modifies the man; whereas an atom goes comparatively stolidly, "impassively" about its business though whole nations groan in agony. Again, a man's complexity is greater than that of an atom, and this is much more obvious than that his integrity or unity is greater.

Aquinas admits this, but pretends that it proves nothing as to complexity in God. However, not only is it true that in all factual cases the higher beings are more complex and more amply passive but the alternative is not even coherently conceivable. Passivity is correlative to activity by the very meaning of the ideas; to act upon another appropriately is to act relatively to the nature and activity of another, and this relativity is passivity. *Passivity is the social relevance of activity,* that which gives activity an object. The effort to escape this leads to such patent incoherences as that God's action upon free will "infallibly" makes us do exactly what we do do, but makes us do it freely, that is, so that we were *not* made to do it but were "free to do something else."

Similar considerations will show that the higher integrity must go with greater variety or complexity, and the uttermost permanence with the supreme capacity for change. Among the arguments for the traditional denial of these correlations, I shall consider one. As the capacity for entertaining good purposes and thoughts increases (the argument runs), that for entertaining bad ones increases also. The more complex and amply passive beings are thus also the more unstable. Satan was a rebel angel, and every angel, I suppose, is a potential Satan. If, then, God is the upper limit of the series of more and more complex and social beings, he must be infinitely fragile and infinitely capable of ill will. This argument I answer briefly as follows. The upper limit of a series must have some unique properties. All that is required is that this uniqueness really follows from, rather than contradicts, the law of the series. Now it is a law of the series of beings that the higher members are more modifiable by others, socially responsive to them, and in this way more complicated in their being. But it follows from this law that the highest being is modifiable and complicated by others in the highest degree, therefore by *all* others, and from this it follows that these others must be its internal members, for an external member is one which, *in so far as it is external,* fails to modify and complicate the being to which it is external. The highest member in the world society will be passive to the other members only as the soul is passive to the body which it dominates, controls, and possesses. The conclusion is that all those aspects of complexity and dependence which derive from relationship to what is external and unpossessed will be absent from the highest activity-passivity. The possibility of ill will and of destruction are just such aspects derivative from an external environment. Where all entities are fully enjoyed and possessed within, there can be no "envy" of others (recall Plato's remark concerning the Creator), no competitive conflict with them; for their being and good must be integral to one's own being and good, more completely than a man's cells are integral to the man, for these cells are only more or less internal to or possessed by the human mind. Thus, for example, the bones are less internal or fully possessed than are the brain cells.

The sociality of existence can then be fully preserved and maximized in God without attributing to him evil will or impermanence. And his maximal dependence or passivity will be compatible with his possessing also maximal independence or absoluteness (in another aspect of his being). Giving and receiving do not conflict with, but supplement, each other. As receiving, God indeed "depends," but for what? Not for his existence, the fact that he is and is himself. This being-himself he has never received. What he receives is rather his being-himself-with-just-this-or-that-content-of-social-experience. It is the essence of personal self-identity, is it not, that it is at least somewhat independent of the detailed content of experience? I can be myself whether to my knowledge you say "Yes" to my previous question or "No." But there are some contents that I could not have in my experience, for example, the observation of my own death or birth. Only God can experience *whatever can* occur, and so only in God is the aspect of independence which is inherent in selfhood an absolute independence—in that aspect. This aspect is that of existence and essential personality. And this not only is compatible with but implies an unrivaled dependence as to exact non-essential content. No other being is so sensitively modifiable by *all* that comes to exist; and none so completely and consciously mirrors all realities other than itself. This mirroring is not merely active, for realities are partly self-determined, and, in determining themselves, they determine what God is to mirror. He does not by mirroring decide that, and just how, they are to exist; for then they would have no reality as self-decided and free.

It has been the contention of many theologians, most recently Nygren, that the divine love is entirely without "need" or "desire" and has nothing to gain from the good it bestows.[8] This is supposed to guarantee the unselfishness of the divine love, whereas (it is thought) the selfish loves, as such, spring from dependence and desire. This, I maintain, is not good religion but bad metaphysics. To will the good of others is the entire positive side of benevolence, and it adds nothing to this to insist that one must *not*, in willing the good of others, find in this good *also* good for one's self. Why, in fact, do we regard human love as imperfect? Is it really because the lover regards the gain of the other as also a gain for himself? Or is it not rather because the wish for self to some extent *con-*

---

3. I have been told that I here misinterpret Nygren's intent, but that "he lays himself open to this misinterpretation." After some discussion with Nygren himself, I am happy to be able to think we are perhaps not far apart. In any case, the following discussion concerns the issue, not any particular theologian.

flicts with, inhibits, and renders precarious the wish for others? The one who loves from a *fluctuating, limited* need to see others prosper will love only so long and so far as the need extends; beyond that he will be indifferent, or he will hate. But suppose the need that others should prosper extends all the way and endures everlastingly, *covering fully all the needs of others?* Suppose it is always and precisely God's need (not as necessary to his existence but to his fullest happiness) that the utmost possible good of the creation be accomplished? Such need obviously could not conflict with the unstinted service of the creature. Surely it is absurd to quarrel with an unflinching and complete devotion to the good of others simply because this good is also a good for self! No pragmatic or operational difference can be imagined between this love and the alleged love without need. What is there but word-idolatry in the traditional insistence upon the latter? And what, on any analogical basis, could be meant by perfect altruism or generosity but a complete finding of one's own good in achieving the good of others?

It is actually imperfect men, not the perfect God, who can reasonably be asked to love where they cannot hope always and wholly to gain from the welfare of the beloved. For men are partly ignorant of the good they accomplish for others, as they are of all things in this complicated world. In some cases they cannot even expect to be alive when the intended happiness of others (such as that aimed at in the making of a will) is realized. But God and God alone can count on always surviving and always knowing fully all that he benevolently accomplishes; and, in respect to value, perfect knowledge is perfect possession. Any emotions of beauty and joy which God enables us to have, become elements in his own all-embracing experience, contributory to the richness of that experience. Each such contribution makes possible for God a unique form of beauty which in no other way could have existed for him. Omniscience thus removes from God the sole reason for that form of altruism which seeks the good of another in partial disregard of whether or not it is good for self. Such altruism is in very truth an imperfection, a glory of the imperfect will as such. It is a glory morally because it is the choice of the greater good over the lesser, in cases where one can do more for the whole, including self, by serving others, without corresponding gain for the self. But it is a metaphysical imperfection, because it implies expected ignorance of the good realized for others. Only through this expected ignorance can there be a non-coincidence between the greater good and the good for self.

Thus, theology may avoid the dangerous situation in which Nygren and many another find themselves of seeing nothing in common or analogous between human love—like that of father for child, or husband for wife, or Jesus for his human fellows—and the divine love. The sublime contrast between human and divine benevolence consists not in the sheer difference between need and no need but in the gap between abysmal ignorance and omniscience, and between *partial and shifting inhibition* of the interest of others by self-interest, as contrasted to *certain and absolute coincidence* of other-interest and self-interest. Most of the good of others is not known to us at all; we *could* not specifically desire it either for their sakes or for ours; and often others' good is just well enough known to us to make apparent its lack of harmony with our own desires. Nevertheless, there is even in us a partial coincidence of desire for self and desire for others; and this is the analogical basis for theism.

The role of *bodily* desire in human love is only an especially striking case of the gap and partial conflict between our felt needs and the needs of others, or our awareness and their good. The body pays little heed, in its demands, to the state of affairs in the lives around it. The body's need is not specifically a need for the creation of good in the lives of those outside the body. But suppose all "others" were within the body, as its members; then, since the need of the body is for the flourishing of its own parts or members, bodily desire and altruism would be coincident. (Even in us bodily desire is in a measure altruistic toward the bodily members.) [4] The idea that the world is, in a manner and analogically speaking, the body of God seems grotesque to us only because we unwit-

4. See my *Man's Vision of God and the Logic of Theism* (Chicago: Willett, Clark & Co., 1941) , pp. 151 ff.

tingly read into it some feature incompatible with the requirement that *all* others be wholly within the body, distinguished
from it as "other" only as members are from the whole, and
the further requirement that this body be *fully possessed* by a
single mind;[5] whereas the human body is not, without qualification, possessed by our minds (for example, much less in
sleep than in waking). This defect of the human body is one
with the fact that this body has an external environment, for
from this it follows that there can be no absolute distinction
between internal and external. Only where nothing is external
can anything be *absolutely* internal. Thus, even a man's brain
cells are not fully possessed by his consciousness (if they were,
we should all be better anatomists than any scientific special-
ist), much less his bones or his fingernails, or the half-
digested food in his stomach.

If we define "desire" as a state of longing whose satisfaction brings joy and whose frustration brings sorrow, or at
least lesser joy, then desire is selfish or unselfish according as
what will satisfy it is, or is not, the very well-being of others
as such. An example of unselfish longing is Lincoln's desire
that the slaves might be free, assuming, as within limits seems
to have been true, that he desired this not primarily that he
might stand forth as the slaves' deliverer but simply that the
slaves and men generally might enjoy a higher level of well-
being. The fact that theologians have thought so little about
the possibility of perfectly generous or other-regarding desire
reflects, one suspects, the poverty of such desires in men. We
must not deny desire to God because, forsooth, if it were *our*
desire it would be niggardly and fitful in its inclusion of the
good of others. What anthropomorphism this is; not less so
because it is in part the result of an over-strained anti-anthro-
pomorphism. If we refuse to conceive God by analogy with
our virtues, that is to say, our other-regarding desires, and
habits of acting upon them, we shall end by conceiving him
by analogy with our vices, for example, our most truly and
deeply "selfish" wish for self-sufficiency—for some mode of
achieving our own good which will release us from the *need*
to achieve the good of others. How the rich and the envious

5. *Ibid.,* pp. 174 ff.

(to some extent all of us) long·to accomplish this trick! To strive to be "independent" in personal self-identity and in *goodness* of character, rightness of volition, is a virtue, and such independence is supreme in God; but the very wish to enjoy, to be happy, altogether independently of others and their happiness or woe, is vicious. In this matter traditional theology is on the side of Satan—or, if you prefer, is at cross-purposes with itself.

Another gift of the new metaphysics to religion is in connection with the problem of immortality. It has often been said that immortal life is now, and is a "quality," not a mere quantitative extension, of living. But what this means, who of the older schools of theology has told us? Yet the social view of reality and of God can tell us. Each of us is, in his very being, his very life just as lived on earth, a contribution to the experience of God. This experience is indestructible; for in order to take on new content God has no need to forget the old. If his attention span were limited in that fashion, he could not, one may argue, fully grasp even the present; for things sum up their histories, and he who has turned his attention away from a thing's past cannot be fully aware of its present. So our least experience, thought, or feeling is an indelible note in the divine symphony. The only question is how far such an element is fortunate for the whole and how far a misfortune. We contribute once for all, every moment, our very being of that moment to the undying treasury of all good. But do we contribute in that moment the *best* we have opportunity for doing, that is, for being, and helping others to be? If so, then we are immortal not only in fact but in quality, that is, we measure up to the dignity of our immortality. This entire account depends upon the social and temporal view of God. For if God received nothing from the events of our lives, then our immortality could consist only in prolongation after death in a new series of adventures. If there be such prolongation, I do not know. But I do know that it would not meet what I must view as the chief need for immortality—the need that our lives, our experiences just as they are, should have permanent value. Apart from a receptive God, the long run significance of our living must be seen in that abstract and highly partial deposit of experience called "character," plus such pale memories as survive in us of our experiences as they become past, along with the hope—desperate enough, at least so far as philosophy or science knows—that death (individual and ultimately racial) will be followed by an endless string of new experiences for each of us. I cannot suppose that we live essentially either merely for the future or for a present which in becoming past becomes virtually nothing, a wraith and an echo; but rather we must live for a present which in becoming past becomes, as Whitehead says, immortal in God, in whom it "lives forevermore." God, according to this faith, is a socially receptive being, taking upon himself the very being of others, contingently upon the manner of their self-determinations, which thereby acquire their abiding significance.

CHAPTER EIGHT

TRAGIC AND SUBLIME ASPECTS
OF CHRISTIAN LOVE

T

HE SOCIAL IMPORTANCE of religious ideas seems
to be dependent upon their embodiment in religious institutions. The Roman Church, as now constituted, is (I fear)
unlikely to accept any such ideas as those which have been presented in previous chapters. There remain, in our part of the
world, the various non-Roman branches of Christianity, and
Judaism. I shall here consider the former only, but with the
hope that some of my remarks will have relevance to the latter
also.

Today, there is much earnest endeavor to mitigate the disunity of the Christian Churches. The attempt to find a common doctrine about God is not, it is recognized, the sole or
perhaps the chief objective of this "ecumenical movement."
Still, few would wholly repudiate such an objective. I believe
that present-day metaphysics can offer some assistance toward
its (never to be wholly complete?) achievement.

As Bernard Iddings Bell has said,[1] the greatest disagreement
in the Christian Church is not between the various churches
—apart at least from the Roman—but between the conservative
and radical wings which are found in nearly every one of them.
There are the orthodox, who stand pat by the doctrines of
their remote ecclesiastical ancestors; and the advanced liberals,
who retain of traditional Christianity little but the name—or
little beyond the idea of human brotherhood—which is common
to many religions, and to many persons without religion in the

---

1. *The Atlantic Monthly,* January, 1946.

usual sense. Is the choice for church people really between those two groups, so hopelessly at odds with each other? One is reminded of the familiar question: shall we uphold "capitalism," with all its traditional traits and defects, or shall we turn to thorough going communism? Most of us, I venture to say, feel and hope, and with increasing clearness definitely think, that much more is to be expected from a "middle way" of some sort—a way which seeks to orchestrate various economic procedures, such as the TVA, consumer's cooperatives, really competitive private enterprise, socially owned monopolies, etc.[2] I wonder if the opposition of orthodox and religious radicals is not similarly an affair of extremes, *between,* rather than *in,* either of which, much of value may lie?

It seems, indeed, that we human beings like the truth somewhat mixed, or wrapped up, with error—rather than plain or "straight." Human mistakes are perhaps seldom pure mistakes, but are more often the wrapping about some truth. So, when we reject as erroneous the views of our forefathers, we should try to remove the wrapping and retain the truth, if there be such, within. This seems especially wise in religious matters, where our modern advantages of science and industry may not be so relevant as elsewhere. When our medieval or colonial forefathers said (as many of our contemporaries still say) that Jesus was God, perhaps they were struggling to say, indirectly and mysteriously, what was not within their power to put directly and literally. If so, what could this have been? Was it merely the "Fatherhood of God," or the "Brotherhood of Man?" Do these rather dull phrases really exhaust the good tidings? If they do, then we may have to conclude that the truth, so far from freeing us for the intensely good life, merely dissipates intensity and delivers us into the bondage of apathy and boredom. God as a superhuman patriarch, a benevolent old gentleman in the sky—to put it crassly—is only mildly inspiring or interesting; and as for human brotherhood, all good men admit it, but most good men also admit—with a sigh—that the mere reminder that men have a common origin and destiny,

---

2. For an excellent discussion of these problems see John Maurice Clark, *Alternative to Serfdom.*

or even a common heavenly Father, gives but little help toward persuading us to deal kindly with one another.

I suggest that much more than divine benevolence or human kinship was symbolized in the doctrine that the man on the cross was deity. The devotion of Jesus to his fellows was not mere benevolence, a wishing them well, or an eagerness to do things for them. It was a feeling of sympathetic identity with them in their troubles and sufferings, as well as in their joys, so that *their* cause and *their* tragedy became his; and he paid the price of a bitter death, rather than weaken the intimacy of his relation to the human lot, with all its suffering and failure. Jesus is a symbol of the solidarity of human weal and woe through sympathy, a solidarity from which the best man will least of all seek to escape. (According to the Fourth Gospel, when Jesus saw the weeping of the friends of Lazarus, he groaned and was troubled in spirit, and wept.) To say that Jesus was God, then, ought to mean that God himself is one with us in our suffering, that divine love is not essentially benevolence—external well-wishing—but sympathy, taking into itself our every grief.

> Oh, he gives to us his joy
> That our grief he may destroy;
> Till our grief is fled and gone
> He doth sit by us and moan.
>
> —*Blake*

In the debate over the divinity of Jesus, this question of a deity who does not escape—or wish to escape—full share in our tribulations, has generally been lost sight of. But is it not perhaps the really important question, of which the other was but an awkward disguise?

Why the disguise, it may be asked? The answer is easy enough. Ancient philosophy and theology attributed to the deity every excellence and denied to him every weakness or defect. But they underestimated the difficulty of discerning what is excellence, and what is defect. Sympathy in man is partly weakness; it may cloud his reason, or paralyze his will. Then, too, sympathy makes the evils of others in some measure also our own, and so it easily comes to us that sympathy is a handicap, not an asset. Instead of thinking, "it is bad that the other should suffer," I tend to think, "the bad thing is that my sympathy should cause his sufferings to become mine." So we are apt to conclude that God must preserve himself from all such contamination with suffering. In this way, while we suppose ourselves to exalt deity we really attribute to him our own subtle selfishness, as well as our feebleness of reason and self-control. *We* cannot control our sympathies so as to render justice to all; therefore God, the just one, must be free from sympathy. But suppose sympathy were omniscient and thus extended to all creatures, in all their aspects—as divine sympathy of course must be—would not then each creature receive his due? It is the one-sidedness, the capriciousness, the instability, the lack of adequacy and proportion, in our human sympathetic responses that make them a source of moral weakness, not their sympathetic character itself. Certain great philosophers and theologians (for example, Whitehead and Niebuhr) have recently accepted the view that God literally suffers. According to this view, when any creature suffers—or rejoices—God is united with that suffering through a sympathy so intimate and absolute that what we call benevolence or love is insignificant, pale, or external, by comparison.

But the cross symbolizes more than divine suffering. It also indicates the root cause of suffering. The world is tragic because the creatures are partly free, within limits making their own choices. A multitude of partly free individuals are bound sometimes to clash, for their choices are made in comparative ignorance of each other, and are thus leaps in the dark, so far as effects upon others are concerned. Unless all were omniscient, this must be the case. But only deity can be omniscient. And if there were only the omniscient, what would the omniscient know, save its own knowing—of what? And upon what would its power be exercised? So it seems that deity needs a world. This world would be insignificant, if even conceivable, were the creatures wholly deprived of their own power, their own self-determination or freedom. There is need for partly free and more or less ignorant beings, which must surely come now and then into conflict with one another. To try so to act that no conflict results is to adjust oneself to fairyland, not any real

world. Indeed, there is plenty of conflict in fairyland, from all
we have heard. What we have to do is to prefer the less deadly,
the more constructive or fruitful, forms of conflict. Thus, we
may tease our trying friend, instead of insulting him.

The cross symbolizes something further. Those who cruci-
fied Jesus were not acting wholly in the dark. The world is
tragic, not only because conflict is inevitable between free and
ignorant beings, but because there is an inner conflict in men
between their will to serve a common good and their desire
to promote a private or tribal goal. Some conflicts are chosen
where a less destructive, more fruitful form of interaction is
known. The crucifying of Jesus, we feel, must have embodied
somewhere, in someone, a deliberate choosing of the greater
evil and the lesser good. This is sin, the supreme tragedy. We
also see, from the Gospel story, that the root of sin is not just
man's animality, his so-called lower nature of physical desires.
No such desire put Jesus on the cross. No, it was the higher
nature corrupted and twisted; it was in the name of God that
the Son of Man was turned over to the Roman crucifiers. He
was a blasphemer. And those who so judged were, they thought,
seeing the matter through God's eyes, as it were, defending the
divine honor. In short, they were, in self-assumed function, the
deity. This self-assumption of divine functions is perhaps the
most basic sin. We can all of us see the possibility of it in ourselves. We should like to seem infallible, omnipotent, absolutely
righteous, at least in some sphere.

Our fathers called the ultimate source of evil in man original sin. According to Mr. Bell, the deepest cleavage among
Christians is over this matter of human depravity. Can man,
apart from God, save himself morally? But does this question
really define a clear issue? To any believer, nothing is simply
"apart from God." God is always actively sustaining all men.
On the other hand, psychiatry—as well as common experience—
shows all of us, save those who will not see, that somehow it is
deeply natural to man to prefer the lesser or narrower to the
greater or more generous objective, and that we can only rise
to our full human stature by availing ourselves of every resource
open to us. Is not the supreme resource the possibility of *consciously and willingly* accepting the operation in us of the love

which infinitely transcends but inspires our own? The humble sense of divine transcendence may come to us easily enough at such times as we remember what the injunction to love one's neighbor as oneself really means. It does not mean, acting benevolently, condescendingly, and simply according to our ideals for the other's welfare. For that is not the way we love ourselves. *We* want to be happy, not according to other people's ideals, but according to our own. So we have to take into account the ideals of others when we pretend to promote their welfare. But how infinitely difficult and complicated this is, and how it goes against the grain sometimes to try sincerely to *do* it! Only God can literally love others with the same intimacy with which he loves himself.

But the sense that we cannot love as God loves, while it humiliates us, may also "save" us from failure to love as we can. To fill one's mind with the thought of the divine, not as coldly perfect or blandly benevolent, but as tragically sympathetic, more at one with us in our grief than we can be with each other, or even with our own past experiences (which we, but not God, have largely forgotten) is to find selfish desires and pride losing some of their charm.

The theory of divine incarnation in Jesus expressed still another religious conception. Jesus was a being whose experiences succeeded each other in time. To all appearances he was no more "immutable" or "timeless" than the rest of us. Moreover, our forefathers declared that the church was the "mystical body" of the life of Christ in history, and that this body is temporal. Each of us, by contributing to the life of the church, contributes to the life of Jesus and so to the life of deity. Modern philosophy has reached a point of view which enables us to take a more direct way to relate our lives in time to the divine life. Formerly, it seemed self-evident that the perfection of God was incompatible with any kind of change, and in addition the Bible seems to say, in so many words and repeatedly, that God does not change. However, the philosophical difficulties, according to most philosophers of the past twenty-five years or so, run rather the other way. It is a God wholly out of time, rather than one in some sense in flux, that has been found difficult if not impossible to render even dimly intelligible.

As for the biblical sayings, even assuming that we accept their literal truth, the context in every case (for example, in Malachi, 3; 6) indicates that the changelessness ascribed to deity refers to his ethical character or his intentions, and not to his total being. The same character or purpose can be expressed differently at different times. So we no longer require the indirect method of attributing real change to deity.

What is the significance of this attribution? The significance is clear and immense. It means that what happens makes a difference to God, that he has a future, and that we help to determine each new stage of the divine life as it becomes real or present. For, by his sympathetic omniscience, our free acts are participated in by God, for weal or woe according to the quality of living which we present to him in these acts. Hence, we can feel that every moment of our lives contributes a unique quality to the divine experience, and the finer the quality the richer the life of God, so far as derived from us. Thus, we find at last an answer to the old question, what does it all matter, since time swallows up each precious joy in the great emptiness of the past. The past, we can now feel, is not empty, but is the inconceivably beautiful and sublime record of all experience in the divine memory. And *we* have made a little of that imperishable beauty, and perhaps also have tinged it imperishably with tragedy.

What is the practical bearing of the foregoing reflections? In a certain great city, veterans and Negroes are in especially desperate need of housing. The cry goes up from property owners, "yes, housing for veterans, perhaps housing for Negroes, but not in *our* neighborhood." Some of these persons are doubtless church people, and probably more of them believe there is a God. But how many have thought to themselves, that it is not just veterans or Negroes that are seeking houses. It is, as many Hindus would put it, God himself that is seeking a home. A Christian should say this as well as a Hindu. "Inasmuch as ye do it unto the least of these . . ." Once more, Christians have symbols which they even yet do not know the meaning of. That other fellow (of whatever social class) whose sonship to God we may abstractly admit, is not just a product of divine power, or just an object of divine well-wishing, but a very fragment of the life of God which is made all-inclusive through sympathy. We ourselves are valuable only because we, too, are caught in the same unity of love. Men seem outside each other, and they imagine they are all outside God; but space is in God, not God merely in space or merely "outside" space (in some super-space?). All is within the divine sympathy. We are members one of another because we are members of the living whole, bound together by solidarity of feeling, a solidarity imperfect in us but perfect and absolute in God. If we even inconvenience our fellows, we inconvenience God; if we torture our fellows, we torture God; as used to be said, we re-crucify Jesus—that is, the God symbolized by Jesus. Well may we "fear" God sometimes. The fear need not be of God's judgment, as implying punishment, but of our own shame in having to agree with that judgment.

Thus, Jesus was, and can still be, a living and unique symbol of the Christian or tragic view of divine love, a symbol taken as deity partly because in this way attention could be diverted from certain difficulties felt to arise if it be said directly that God sympathizes, suffers, and changes. The difficulties no longer seem so acute or invincible, and on the other hand, it seems to many of us that such difficulties as there are can only be increased by joining the two statements, "God does not suffer or change in any fashion," and, "Jesus, who suffers and changes, is God."

Although I believe the doctrine of the Incarnation enshrined important religious truth, I feel in honesty bound to add the following. I very much doubt if there ever has been or ever can be a form of theism which will enable such phrases as "Jesus was God" or the "divinity of Jesus" to have a sufficiently unambiguous meaning to entitle them to serve as requirements for Christian unity. The most they can do is to name a mystery which is felt rather than thought; and people may well feel differently about different ways of phrasing the mystery. The ambiguity spoken of is double. On the one hand, no one can be man and *in every sense* also God. This would be no mystery, but simple contradiction. To be God is, for example, to know all things; to be man is to know in limited fashion (as more or less bounded by senses and discursive inference). To assert both

unqualifiedly of the same subject is merely to talk nonsense. On
the other hand, if it is only in *some* sense that Jesus was God,
then we must remember that in some sense or degree every man
is God. He is an expression of the divine life, as are all things
whatever (even though not all are in accord with the divine
ideal for them). Thus, it seems probable that any doctrine of
the divinity of Jesus must do one of the following: (1) assert
and deny the same predicates of one logical subject; (2) assert
the truism that a certain man (like all things, but more richly
or purely than others) is a manifestation of divine love; or
(3) leave it indeterminate, uncertain, or vague as to what, between these useless extremes, is asserted. Possibly one could
define a sufficiently distinctive sense in which, without contradiction, Jesus could have been both God and man; but, unless
and until this can be done, to make acceptance of the phrases in
question a test of being a Christian is unwittingly to make a
low degree of intellectual penetration—or honesty—an important factor in religious correctness. Is this what is really desired?

Our medieval forefathers had two great symbols for God,
the Incarnation, and the doctrine of the Trinity. The latter had
the function of ascribing an inner social life to the deity, a love
of God for God. It also mitigated the sense of emptiness that
afflicts us when we try to think of deity as wholly unitary, or
as the technical term ran, "simple." Finally, through the professed incomprehensibility of the doctrine, a sense of sublime
mystery and of the limitations of the human mind was given
expression. These functions can all be more directly served in
another way. If God is in process, then he has, in a sense, a distinct personality for each stage of his life. Each such stage loves
its predecessors as also divine, as we sympathize with our past
selves (to the slight and far from divine extent to which we are
able to be aware of them). And each divine stage looks forward
to its successors (not seeing these as distinct and settled items—
for they are not that—but as possibilities whose exact form of
actual realization will be determined only when the time comes,
and then partly by the free acts of creatures). But how about
the sense of mystery and of human limitation? Well, for *three*
persons, we have substituted *infinity,* as the number of past
selves of deity in a process which we must, it seems, conceive

as beginning-less. (And if we tried to conceive a beginning, that, too, surely would escape our comprehension!) Now if "three in one" was mysterious, is "infinite number in one" so plain and prosaic?

In a certain way, the number three has also its point, even for such a theology as I have been sketching. For a deity in process has an aspect of the settled past, of the to-be-determined future, and of the abstract "character" of "divinity," for example, the general quality of perfect sympathy, which makes God always God, through all the novelties of his experience. Some of the old attempts to construe the Trinity are not wholly diverse from this. Certainly, the past has something analogous to the Father, the future to the Son, and the identity of divine purpose through all changes to the Holy Spirit, with the present, the concrete actuality or "substance" in which all of these are contained.

Contemporary Christianity has the choice among three, not two, basic possibilities. (1) It may simply continue in the line of orthodoxy. (2) It may reject *in toto* both the orthodox doctrines of the Incarnation and of the Trinity. (3) It may extract from these doctrines the conceptions of man and God which they seem to have had the function to express, under the limitations of ancient philosophy and literalistic Biblicism. Church unity may depend ultimately upon whether and when Trinitarians are willing to unwrap their spiritual treasures from ancient errors, and anti-Trinitarians (including eventually, even those of Jewish faith?) are willing to receive the treasure thus laid bare.

CHAPTER NINE

THREE IDEAS OF GOD

I N THE HUNDRED YEARS since Darwin was a young man, science has made immense advances. Its most fundamental conceptions have been altered and clarified. During this same period theology also has made advances, though of these the public has been less well informed. It has been found that the conception of God upon which, with all their quarrels over details, theologians used to agree, is not the only possible conception, nor even the best one, for either religious or philosophical purposes. There are, indeed, three and, from one point of view, only three chief ways of thinking about God. The *first* is that God is in all respects perfect and complete. This means He cannot change, or grow, or in any way increase in value. Therefore nothing man can do can bring any additional values to God. In that case, what does it mean to talk of serving God? This is only one of the embarrassing questions which can be asked of this type of theology. The *second* view of God is that he is perfect and complete in some respects, but not in all. For instance, he may be perfect in goodness, or in love; but not in happiness. Never changing in his righteousness, he might yet grow in joy as his creatures served him, and themselves grew in joy. Is it so strange to say that one who loves perfectly is yet made happier by the increasing welfare of those he loves? Would it not rather be very strange if God, who loves us, gained no new joy from our achievements and growth? The *third* way of thinking about God is that he is not in any respect entirely perfect. It would follow that there is no way in which he could not change. This would deprive the idea of God of most of its value, for one could place no ultimate reliance upon a deity in every way subject to imperfection and alteration.

It is certain that God, if he is to be conceived at all, and if "perfect" means anything, must be supposed one of the three: perfect in all ways, perfect in some ways, or perfect in no way. If he is perfect in all ways, and if perfect means complete and incapable of enhancement, then the greatest saint can do no more for God than the worst sinner, for neither could possibly add to, or subtract from, what is always wholly perfect. And such a God could not love in a real sense, for to love is to find joy in the joy of others and sorrow in their sorrows, and thus to gain through their gains and lose (or at least, miss some possible value) through their losses, and the wholly perfect could neither gain nor lose. Hence, it could not love in a proper sense. On the other hand, if God is perfect in no way, then he would scarcely deserve our worship, religion would have certainly overpraised him, and we could not rely upon him. Thus, only the second possibility is left, that God is *perfect in love,* but never-completed, *ever growing* (partly through our efforts) in the joy, the richness of his life, and this without end through all the infinite future.

Until recently no one, apparently, ever saw clearly that there are these three ways, and (apart from subdivisions of each) just these three, of conceiving God, and it is also only recently that the advantages of the second way over the first, or most usual, way as well as over the third, have been at all widely appreciated. This is as definite an advance in thought as anything we owe to Einstein or Darwin. It is a rather simple change, but so is the idea of evolution fairly simple. There is this difference, that the man in the street, or in the parlor listening to the radio, has a better chance of grasping the evidence upon which the new theological doctrine rests than he has of appreciating Darwin's arguments, to say nothing of Einstein's. Anyone can see that a purely perfect, complete, self-sufficient deity can have nothing to ask of us, for there is nothing we could give him. *We* might have things to ask of him, but even this would be senseless, for why should he think it mattered about us, since whatever happens to us his life contains all possible joy and value, and, therefore, existence as containing this sum of possible values would lack nothing if we did not even exist.

It is not surprising that men have reacted against this idea of God. Nor is it surprising that at first they went to the opposite extreme, and denied the existence of God (as in any way perfect) altogether. The human mind seems to have to work in this way. It begins by an over simplification, such as that God is simply and without qualification perfect. If this leads to difficulties, as it does, then the opposite simplification is tried: God —if there is any being worthy of the name—is wholly imperfect, there is no being who could, even with qualifications, be called perfect. Only at long last, does it dawn on men that the problem is not so simple, that the mere denial and the mere assertion of perfection may both be wrong, since the truth may lie in the combined assertion and denial of a perfect being according as perfection is taken in different sense.

To say God is perfect may be defined to mean that he is better than any possible individual other than himself. This leaves open the possibility that, though no individual who is not God can be better than he, still he himself might improve. Unsurpassable by others, he might yet surpass himself, might grow in value. To conceive God as capable of improvement in *goodness* shocks the religious sense, which feels that God could not possibly be more just or merciful than he is. In ethical quality and in wisdom and power, religion conceives God as already as perfect as anything could be. But does religion assure us that God is equally incapable of improvement in happiness? How can this be if God loves us, and through love shares in our sorrows, and is grieved by our misfortunes and errors? But even here we may call God perfect, if we mean by this that he is not to be surpassed in happiness by any being other than himself. To say God can increase in happiness (and if he cannot, then there is no service we can render him) is not to say that any other individual is or could be happier than he, but only to say that he himself could be happier. In other words, if perfect means supreme among individuals, then God is in all respects perfect; but if perfect means incapable of growth or improvement, then only in goodness, wisdom, and power is God perfect.

Thus, we see how carefully perfection must be defined. And similar care must be exercised with respect to other conceptions commonly applied to God, such as that he is immutable, unchanging. In goodness he is for religion indeed ever the same, as he is in wisdom and power. But love is more than goodness, wisdom, and power, it is also happiness as partly arising from sympathy with the joys of others. This happiness will of course change with changes in the joys of others. But does not God see in advance all the joys that will ever exist? Is he not all-knowing? It has been shown that this argument, plausible as it is, is fallacious. For to know all that is, is not necessarily to know all future events; for the question is, do future events exist? Is it not the essence of the future that it consists of what may or may not exist, that is, of what is unsettled, indefinite, undecided? If so, then God, who knows things as they are, will know future events only in their character as indefinite, or more or less problematic, nebulous, incomplete as to details. Thus, the very great discovery has been made (dating indeed from the fourteenth century, but neglected until recently) that omniscience does not mean the total absence of growth or change. What is now unsettled, both in itself and for God, may become settled, and as it does so he will acquire new content for his happiness as derived from sympathy with the creatures.

The old theology was a first approximation; like Newtonian science it was an oversimplification. All its conceptions are true, provided they are qualified as theologians have only recently learned to qualify them.

We live in a world in which brute force looms large. That may make it more difficult to believe in a divine, a perfect love; but it also makes it more important to do so. It is a strange fate that has overtaken man during the last two thousand years. Having reached the sublime idea of divine perfection, he failed to see that it is impossible to be perfect in love without being other than absolutely perfect in enjoyment. For to love is to find joy in the joys of others, and sorrow in the sorrows of others, and thus to depend partly upon them for one's joy and sorrow. And the ideal of love is so hard for men to understand that they forgot that the perfection of God is the perfection of *love,* and began to think of God as simply perfect in general; and so, without knowing it, they spoiled the conception of divine love. Naturally, the result was that many men drifted away from any idea of God at all, and today millions can find no better ideal than that of arbitrary power. Fortunately for the world the root of the difficulty has been discovered. Great philosophers like Bergson and Whitehead, theologians like Tennant, James Ward, Pfleiderer, Macintosh, Calhoun, Berdyaev, and many others, have been clarifying the relations between love and perfection in God, and I believe that never again will it be possible for generation after generation of leaders of thought calmly to take it for granted that God must be conceived as motionless in pure perfection and self-sufficiency, incapable of receiving anything from man, or of being served by man in any real sense, incapable of anything that ever has been meant by love.

The idea that God's power must be limited, imperfect, is not very new, but it is only recently that men have seen that it is God's happiness, not his power, that must be less than "perfect" if the word means, "incapable of increase." For it is possible to explain evil in the world through the free action of agents other than God, but no explanation can make sense out of the idea of a will which has purposes yet lacks nothing pleasurable which it might seek to attain, a mind which knows a changing world yet itself suffers no change, which knows free beings whose action is undetermined in advance yet knows determinately what their actions will be, a mind subject to no risks although its creatures act on their own responsibility and with limited wisdom, and though it loves these creatures, cares for their welfare, and hence must mentally share in their fortunes, good or bad.

A God both perfect and, in other ways, imperfect (save as perfection is defined, as was suggested above, to mean "surpassing all others") can change, whereas a being wholly perfect could change neither for the better nor for the worse. The objection to a God in all ways imperfect would be that he could in all ways change, and hence might cease to be recognizable at all, might lose its individual identity altogether. The objection to a God in all ways perfect (in the old sense) would be that it could in no way change, and hence while it could not lose its identity, it also would not have any significant identity to lose. For we know individual identity as identity through change, and if change is simply omitted from our idea of God, nothing conceivable is left. A changeless being can have no purposes, for purposes refer to the future and the future is related to the present by change. A changeless being cannot love, for to love is to sympathize with, and through sympathy to share in, the changes occurring in the persons one loves.

Since perfection cannot change, and imperfection cannot be changeless, it follows that a God *both* perfect and imperfect will be unchanging in the ways in which he is perfect, and changing in the ways in which he is not perfect,. If, as religion says, God is perfect in goodness, wisdom, and power, then he is unchanging in these respects. Is this not what the Bible means when it says God is without shadow of turning? His goodness of purpose will never alter in the slightest. But where in the Bible are we told that God never becomes *happier*, from time time? We are not told so. What has religion to lose by the idea that God is made happier (though not more wise or good) by the successes of men; as well as grieved by their failures or wickedness? Surely religion has nothing to lose by this idea. Yet until recently nearly all the theologians in the world spoke of God as incapable of any kind of change, even change in his happiness?

Does it not make God more real to us to think of him as subject to change, as like us in having purposes for the future, memories of the past, and the power to receive additions to his happiness?

The memory of God is an inspiring idea. We say the past is gone. What does this mean? Where has it gone to? If the past were gone in the sense of now not existing at all, how could anything we say of it be true, for can a true statement be about what does not exist at all, that is, about nothing real? Surely, the landing of the Mayflower at Plymouth exists somehow in the universe, or when we speak of it we are merely talking about a dream. And it must exist now, for our statement is true now, and how can a relation be real when the thing it relates to is unreal? Now memory is the way we experience the past as real in the present, to the extent of the memory. Our memory is so feeble that the events we remember are not fully preserved for us by the fact that we remember them. But the events we best remember are the ones most nearly preserved as still real. I can remember a certain won-

derful moment so well that the beauty of it is almost fully
embodied in the present by that memory. Now if God changes
but has perfect knowledge, then all the past must still be
before him without loss of any detail or quality in the present;
that is, he must have perfect memory. From this memory no
joy once attained anywhere in the world can ever be lost.

You may ask, "Must God not have perfect anticipation of
the future also?" But I answer that anticipation is a different
thing from memory, and what makes it different is that it
does not even want to be perfect in the same sense as memory
would like to be. Our relation to the past is purely that of a
spectator. We can do nothing about the past, it has been what
it has been, and no power can alter the fact that it has been
so. But the future is what we are engaged in deciding, it is
our sphere of choice and action. Therefore, it is not the function of anticipation to decide exactly what will happen; that
function is for the *will*, the practical side of the mind. If you
were to anticipate with certainty what your future decisions
will be, you would have made these decisions already! The
business of anticipation is to ascertain the *limits of choice*.
You may have power to decide between saying "hello" and
saying "howdy" when we meet, and if this is to be a genuine
decision made at that moment neither you nor I will know
in advance with certainty which you will say. But we may
either or both of us be able to anticipate, as at least probable,
that you will address me in English, or that you will address
me in French, if you do not know English. The role of anticipation is to narrow down the range of possibility in general, or of what is conceivably abstractly, to that group of
possibilities whose realization is possible, not simply in general, but at some specified future date, and with a certain
degree of probability. Anticipation *grades* possibilities, so
that action can take account of the most probable lines of
action, and try to bring about the one that is most desirable.

Even God's anticipation would have reference to action as
choice among probabilities. He would not see what "is to
happen," but the range of possible things among which what
happens will be a selection. And he will see that a higher per-
centage of some kinds of things will happen than others, that

is, he will see in terms of probabilities. This seems to be the only view of God's knowledge that does not make human freedom impossible, or that does not destroy the religious idea of God as perfect in goodness and wisdom.

The view is also not an utter novelty. It was defended by Levi ben Gerson, in the fourteenth, and (more clearly and consistently) by Fausto Socinus in the sixteenth century. It was, however, not to be expected that a Jew and an anti-Trinitarian could in those times secure favorable consideration for their doctrines. Today there is no reason why they should not be considered on their merits.

CHAPTER TEN

TWO LEVELS OF
FAITH AND REASON

A PHILOSOPHY THAT ISSUES in religious conceptions cannot evade the ancient problem of the relations of faith and reason. "Faith" in general is trust, and this means, doing our part in the system of things with confidence that the rest of the system will do its part, at least to the extent that we shall not have striven simply in vain. What Santayana calls "animal faith" is the confidence of every sentient creature in its environment as favorable to its efforts to live and continue its species. Faith on the human level is trust that the nature of things insures the appropriateness of ideals of generosity, honesty, and esthetic refinement, or goodness, truth, and beauty, to such an extent that despite all frustrations and vexations, despite disloyalty or crassness in our fellows, despite death itself, it is really and truly better to live, and to live in accord with these ideals, than to give up the struggle in death or in cynicism. Of this human faith there are varieties almost beyond telling: the great religious faiths, and the various attempted philosophical substitutes for these.

Reason in general is either a mere tracing of the consequences of ideas, whether true or false, that is, mere deduction, as in mathematics, or an attempt to estimate the truth of ideas by the honest weighing of evidence, the most accurate attainable estimation of pros and cons. This weighing of evidence has two main forms or levels: the inductive reasoning of science and everyday life; and the presumed reasoning, not easy to classify, which is at work in the construction of systems of metaphysics and theology.

[163]

We can now render our question of the relation of faith to reason somewhat more definite, as follows: how are the processes of deduction, and of weighing of evidence (on the two levels mentioned), related to trust in the environment as an adequate basis for our efforts to live in accordance with certain ideals? At once, we note that deducing consequences of ideas, and weighing evidence for ideas, are themselves modes of behavior, and of these modes, as of any others, we must ask, what is their ideal, and is the world such that this ideal is practicable? For if it is not, why should we bother to study mathematics or to pursue inductive science or metaphysics? As has been often remarked, the entire life of man, including quite especially his intellectual life, is the expression of faith or trust, for example, trust that the human discovery of truth is possible and worth striving for. Since this is the case, there is an absurdity in supposing that faith is unjustified until and unless it can find evidence to support it. To look for evidence is to express one's trust in the value of evidence. The most basic animal and human faith is beyond need of justification. Even suicide expresses the trust that to die is, in certain cases at least, better than to live. What needs justification is not faith in general, for to think, as to live, is already to accept faith as valid. What needs justification is only the choice of *which* faith, which verbal and intellectual and perhaps institutional, ritualistic, and artistic form of expression and intensification we shall seek to give the faith we inevitably have. Here truly we do need justification, not merely by faith, but of faith. Is there any way to achieve this, if not by deducing the consequences of various interpretations of the content of faith, and examining the arguments for and against each? The only alternative is to put unlimited trust in our luck in having been born into the right religion, or in our capacity to make the right choice without any careful consideration of relevant arguments.

In the comparison of diverse faiths, reason asks us to be technically neutral; that is to say, whatever may be the particular form of faith we happen to incline to, we ought to reason as if we had no such inclination. It is obvious that nothing is humanly more difficult than to achieve such neutral-

ity of reasoning. Here—as Niebuhr points out—is a mighty
ambiguity in the term "reason." It means one thing so far as
it designates an ideal of thinking, and something more or less
radically different so far as it stands for this or that man's
practice of thinking. The ideal neutrality which reasoning
calls for is only an ideal, so far as man is concerned. He tries
to play fair as between the faith he would like to justify and
rival faiths, but scarcely can he ever wholly succeed. Here is
the element of truth in the disparagement of "reason" often
expressed by men of faith. What we actually have is not reason
but various alleged reasonings. They are genuine reasonings
so far as evidences and counter-evidences are both honestly
considered, but for the rest they are pseudo-reasonings, pre-
tences to face evidence where the reality is lacking. But
granted all this, are not the men of faith in the same human
boat along with the rest of us? If they renounce reason in
favor of resting content with their own form of faith, on
what ground do they claim validity for this form? If they
say, we have received it directly or indirectly from God himself who cannot deceive or be in error, the question is, by
what mode of human response to a divine message could
the possibility of error be ruled out? If alleged reasonings
are often pseudo-reasonings, alleged receptions of revealed
messages are often pseudo-receptions, as is proved by their
mutual disagreements, and in other ways. And if it be said,
ah! but original sin and the fall of man condemn human
thinking to perversion, must this not be at least as true of
human reception of divine revelation? The message is divine,
but we miserable human wretches must receive and interpret
it if it is to become our own living faith.

In at least one sense, however, it seems correct to say that
faith transcends rational justification. After we have weighed
the evidences as best we can, the question is: how conclusive
is the result? Rational neutrality may remain at the end as it
is obligatory at the beginning of the process. And yet a living
faith we need, and something more definite than the mere
general faith that somehow it is all right for us to live and
try to do our best. Such complete vagueness is not practicable,
and it means that the content of the word "best" also remains

all too vague. So it seems that each individual must carry on such reasoning as he has opportunity and leisure to effectuate, and then "take a chance" on the best guess he can make. His reasoning may seem to favor this faith over that, but inconclusively. Yet his life of faith can hardly be equally undecided. Or can it? And is such indecision desirable? At least, it should, as Niebuhr says, survive in our practical faith in the form of tolerance. Since I am not rightfully certain, I cannot set down the disagreements of others with me as simply so many errors. I may practice my own ritual with cheerful confidence, but I ought not to condemn you uncharitably, or with a sense of personal infallibility, for similarly practicing yours. And I ought not to condemn myself too definitively, or my children, to persistence in that ritual unchanged, should new evidences become apparent to me.

There are two chief areas in which the relations of the various faiths with reason are today critical. There is the area of contact between faith and contemporary metaphysics, and that of contact between faith and the social sciences. Not being a social scientist, I hesitate to discuss the second of these areas. Lundberg's *Can Science Save Us?* states the problem brillliantly (though one-sidedly), and should be widely read by theologians. Certainly it will not do to say that science merely invents machines and only faith can tell us how to use these machines. For psychology, psychiatry, anthropology, sociology, scientific history, seem to tell us a good deal about the men who use machines, and can we know how men may best act if we do not know what men are, or can we know what God wishes us to do if we do not know what he has created us to be, or what, by using the freedom of choice with which he has endowed us, we have made of ourselves? I do not doubt that Dewey's constant refrain, let religious leaders stop sabotaging the efforts of social science to clarify our ideals, or let people cease to give heed to religious leaders, has enough justification to deserve more hearing than Niebuhr, for example, is willing to admit. Since the ideal of reason calls for devotion to norms of correct intellectual procedure as having pre-eminence over personal preference, and since the basic ideal of religion is selflessness, setting of super-personal values above self-interest and self-will, religious persons should see in social science one of the chief opportunities to exemplify religious idealism.

The contact between faith and metaphysics is a difficult, complex topic. Is metaphysics a genuine expression of reason, or are its arguments only pseudo-reasonings? I believe that metaphysics is, in ideal possibility, a genuine expression of reason, but that in historical achievement it has in good part been a failure. However, it may be questioned if revealed or orthodox theology is in better case, or is justified in scorning metaphysics. For (not to mention the competing orthodoxies) I hold that among the most successful of the efforts of metaphysicians are those which go to prove the erroneousness of certain elements in the main stream of orthodox theology, Protestant as well as Roman. Modern philosophy, with increasing unanimity and emphasis, declares that whatever the highest truth may be, it is not to be found in certain theological tenets for which almost innumerable theologians in various churches have stood. There has, in fact, been a basic revolution in metaphysics, quite as noteworthy as the revolution in physics. I shall try to explain.

In medieval doctrine the outstanding illustrations of faith as compared to reason were seen in the doctrines of the Trinity and the Incarnation. That God is, and that he is all-knowing and supremely good, with still other attributes, could, it was held, be rationally known. But that there are three persons in the one divine substance, and that the man Jesus and the second person of the Trinity were also somehow one, though with two natures, one human and one divine, these were truths which must be taken on trust in the authority of Church and Scriptures. What is the situation today? I think it is this: philosophy is indeed sadly divided as to the rational knowability of deity, but on one thing there is as much agreement as on any, that among the attributes which the schoolmen regarded as rationally demonstrable, are some which are at least as recalcitrant to reason as the Trinity or the Incarnation. That God should be the perfection of wisdom and goodness, yet in all respects infinite, changeless, and absolute, this is if anything a more hopeless rebuke to all our rational insights than that there should be threefold personality in God. Wisdom and goodness are essentially relationships, and the wholly nonrelative or pure absolute can in no intelligible sense, know or intend anything; more obviously, if possible, it cannot love anything. Moreover, if God were wholly absolute and immutable, he would be less, not more, rich in fullness of being than if he were relative and mutable; for modern analysis has shown, more and more clearly, that the relative includes the absolute and more besides, and that becoming includes being as well as something additional. We have come to see that by abstracting from relations and change we can indeed conceive the absolute and the changeless, but only as something abstract and deficient in actuality or concreteness. The concrete God that metaphysics finds reason to accept must be described as supreme both in relativity and in absoluteness, both in becoming of novel value and in permanence of values once achieved, both in activity and in passivity, both in simplicity and in complexity. The concrete includes the abstract, and since the absolute or immutable is abstract, it can perfectly well constitute an aspect of a being which concretely or as a whole is relative and mutable.

But granting, as some perhaps would, the conceivability of such a view, can its truth be established? Here we come to the question of the arguments for the existence of God. It is said that such arguments seem cogent only to those largely convinced already. But here there is danger of converting: "It never has been done" into "It cannot be done." It is unsafe to assume that no argument for theism can ever be more cogent than those in Thomas Aquinas or in Royce—or than those set up in order to be demolished by Hume and Kant, or than the moral argument which Kant accepts. It was ages before men learned to reason well in natural science. There are problems in the logic of mathematics, and also in the logic of induction, that are not yet fully solved. I see no reason to suppose and good reason to doubt that Aquinas, Kant, or Royce were equipped to achieve finality in the exploration of the logic of the theistic problem. Metaphysics shows signs of having a future as well as a past, and as Maxwell remarked of physics, we cannot assume that the science of the future—including, I would add, metaphysical science—will be a mere magnified image of that of the past. I believe there are no fewer than six arguments for God which are capable of being so formulated as to eliminate the gravest weaknesses which critics have found in older formulations. They may still not be coercive demonstrations, but there is something between absolute demonstration—as in mathematics—and no rational evidence at all. If the logic of natural science has proved so difficult, how do we know that the logic of metaphysics is easier to master? Perhaps even logical positivism, in spite of itself, will furnish us with tools of analysis which will strengthen rather than weaken the theistic argument as theists learn to use these tools.

Let us return to the conception of God which I have attributed to the new metaphysics. (Since it is possible to read the doctrine into Plato and Schelling, it is new only in the relative sense in which philosophical conceptions are likely to have novelty.) From the current metaphysical point of view, the doctrines of the Incarnation and the Trinity acquire a new meaning. If God has a genuinely relative and mutable aspect, he can genuinely and literally love his creatures. It follows that a man Jesus whose life exemplifies and symbolizes love in uniquely impressive fashion can, at least in some sense (possibly in a rather attenuated one), be said to incarnate or at least symbolize the nature of deity. But further, if there is a real distinction between what is relative and what is absolute in deity, then simple monotheism, which denies all such complexity or internal difference in God, is mistaken. Also, there is a sense in which the new metaphysics implies a plurality of divine persons in the life of God. For if there is divine becoming as well as divine being, then in some real sense God is a new being every moment of his life, and since he is really a knowing and loving being, this succession of beings in God is in a sense a succession of persons. However, the number of such divine persons would presumably be infinite, not three. On the other hand, threefoldness would also remain valid, though in another sense. For besides the absolute element in deity there would be two other elements or aspects. These are: the relative element as such, that is, the generic quality of divine relativity; but also the specific divine relationships to specific actual things or world states. Only the last would constitute God as concrete at a given moment, and in this concrete state of God the two abstract or generic elements would be contained. Thus, there would, at a given moment, be the one concrete deity or divine actuality ("substance") containing three aspects, one of which is the actuality itself in its fullness, while the other two are abstract elements of this actuality. How far these three could be identified with the Father, Son, and Holy Ghost, I suspect is a matter for fancy more than argument, since historical definitions of the three persons contain too many ambiguities, or are too vague, to make such argument much more than a pastime. But this much seems metaphysically justifiable in the Trinitarian doctrine, that there is one divine actuality with three aspects, and that there is a plurality of divine persons in the divine life. Thus, the empty bleakness of mere unity, mere undifferentiated perfection, is overcome as well, or rather, much better, in the new doctrine than in the old.

It is important to note that the language of religion is not precise with reference to philosophical problems. In about four places in the Bible God is said to be unchanging. So Jews and Christians might suppose that their religion commits them to the philosophical tenet of an immutable deity. But this is open to question. Suppose I say to a friend, I met so and so. And my friend says to me, how is he? And I say, just the same as ever. Do I literally and precisely mean what I say? Of course not. No man is ever in every respect the same at two different times. What I mean is that so and so exhibits certain traits of character that are constant. Now how do we know that the biblical writers meant that God in no sense whatever changes? Perhaps they only meant that certain traits of character, of great importance to religion, are absolutely constant and therefore wholly to be relied upon in God, say his righteousness or his wisdom. It need not follow that God in no sense or respect changes, even in those which perhaps would make no difference to religion, or might even be favorable to it.

It is for philosophy and religion together to work out the possible senses in which deity may be conceived as changing, in spite of a certain unchangeability of character.

One cause for the erroneous view that God is "without accidents" is that his very existence must, it seems, be an accident if his actual being contains accidental factors. But this, once more, is a confusion between abstract and concrete. *That* God is concrete or actual is, I hold, necessary, but *how* he is actual, in what contingent concrete state rather than another, is not necessary. The point is that nonexistence is not a possible state or accident of God. God can be in *any* contingent state, save the pseudo-state of not existing, that is, of not realizing *somehow* his eternal essence of supreme wisdom, goodness, and power.

The traditional problems of faith and reason are indeed profoundly transformed by the new metaphysics which posits in God a relative, contingent, temporal aspect and holds that this aspect is the concrete actuality of deity. But, you may say, if rational metaphysics can go so far, what of the mysteriousness of God? Surely we cannot understand him? In the first place, metaphysics is reason at its problematic limits. It is mysterious enough. In the second place, reason deals with the universal and abstract; the wholly particular and concrete can only be intuited. Thus, in so far as faith, or life-trust, has something particular as its object it transcends rational evidence. Now each man has to have a sense of his own particular value in the universe and for God, and this no science and no metaphysics can give him, but only his own awareness of himself, and of the world or God as containing him. Rational theology may be able to show that there is a God who cherishes all his creatures; but no rational discipline can show there is a God who cherishes "me," meaning by me, the precise individual quality, incommunicable in abstract terms, that makes me different from anyone else that ever lived or ever could have lived. That about God which reason cannot know is not the essence of God, that which he is in general terms, such as all-knowing, or loving; but the particular form that this knowing or loving takes when a given particular creature is its object. Not the essence, but the most particular of the accidents of God have to be felt rather than demonstrated, if we can know them at all. Even God's relation to the human race is outside the province of metaphysics and must either be deduced from anthropological data, or from the depths of personal intuition, one's own or someone else's.

This whole matter was misconceived for centuries, for at least two reasons: God was thought to have an essence which forbade that he have accidents, anything additional to his eternal and inevitable being, anything temporal or non-necessary; further, it was thought that metaphysics could support only some of the essential attributes which religion ascribes to God. For instance, it was thought that we might know metaphysically the immateriality of God, but not that he is loving or personal. The newer metaphysics holds that it is the general essence of God that he have particular accidental properties which must be transcendent to metaphysical reasoning; on the other hand, lovingness and personality are seen to be just as well supported by metaphysical reasoning as any other attributes. Even the great message of the cross, that the divine suffers, is a truism for metaphysics as I conceive it. It *could not* be that an inclusive mind excluded the suffering of the world from itself. Nothing is more irrational than the notion of an all-knowing mind that does not know suffering, in the only conceivable way in which suffering can be known—by feeling it. In order to have the idea of a divine presence in our human suffering there is no need that metaphysics be supplemented by revelation. What escapes metaphysical reason is something that cannot even be stated in purely general abstract terms, like "suffering" or "personality." Such, for example, are the particular forms of suffering which are yours or mine, or the sufferings of a certain remorseful sinner, and the particular response of feeling to these particular sufferings which takes place in God. Aside from the metaphysically knowable essence of God there are, then, two main aspects of religious truth: first, the accidents of God—in relation to the world as itself accidental—so far as these accidents are abstractly knowable, and second, these accidents so far as they are too concrete or particular to be accessible except to incommunicable intuition or perhaps poetic and artistic, but not conceptual, expression.

The abstractly knowable accidents are in principle open to scientific inquiry. Thus, if God forgives man his sins, anthropology and metaphysics together should be able to make some sense out of this proposition and find some evidence for it. But what *my* sins may be, which God forgives, surely no science will ever quite know that! The reason-transcending aspect of faith is the intimate, particular, personal aspect of the relations of man and God. Now to say, "God is a person and has personal relations," is to talk in abstract general terms, and to betray no personal secrets whatever. Can we not distinguish between the quite impersonal proposition, God is a person, and the revelation of a particular personal act or decision of God in reference to a particular creature? To say, "there are intimacies," is not to reveal any intimacy, any more than to say there are secrets is to let any cat out of the bag.

In sum, metaphysical reason can know the general nature or eternal essence of God; scientific reason can know some of the accidents of God in their more abstract aspect; personal intuition, aided by poetry, ritual, religious traditions, can know some aspects of the accidents of God too concrete, complex, or particular to be grasped by rational analysis. No doubt the aspects of God that we can know by any means are incomparably less extensive than those we cannot know (for instance those referring to the remote depths of the universe in space and time).

Even the most concrete and personal knowledge is not wholly beyond reason. It is hard to set absolute limits to analysis and intersubjective verification. We can always try, and we ought to try, to carry them further into the citadel of the concrete and particular. And in all cases faith should respect and include reason, not flout it. We may even say that any legitimate faith on the human level is a form of reason. For if reason is the critical or honest evaluation of evidence, then faith is the evaluation of evidence too personal to be utilized in science. We may, thus, even speak of secular and sacred reason; the one is the honest weighing of publicly accessible evidence, the other, the similar weighing of evidence available only to certain persons or groups—if you will, those who have received special divine grace.

Included in the criterion of honest weighing of evidence is the requirement of consistency. No evidence, public or private, can support a contradiction, as such. For this would simply mean that the evidence confirms and also disconfirms a certain proposition, and that would amount to saying that we have no idea what the evidence confirms. Those, for example, who think to exalt God by saying that he is in all respects without accidental properties, yet that he has infallible knowledge of accidental beings, fail to tell us what proposition they claim the right to believe in. For to know that that exists which might not have existed is to have knowledge that might not have been had, that is, it is to have accidental knowledge. Suppose what might not have existed had not existed, surely then the infallible knower would not have known that it did exist, for this would have been to know falsely. So this sort of theologizing only amounts to saying, evidence, profane or sacred, gives us the right to believe that there is an infallible knowledge of accidental being and that there is no such knowledge—and this can only mean that the evidence gives us no right to believe either proposition. The question, "what do you claim the right to believe?" is really left unanswered.

I have assumed so far in this paper that metaphysics is an expression of reason, is a legitimate rational enterprise. But if this assumption is really sound, why is distrust of metaphysics so widespread? There are many reasons, but, I hold, no conclusive justification for this distrust. One reason is the question-begging argument, the inductive method has given us all our dependable knowledge, hence metaphysics, which is not inductive, is not dependable. In the first place, it is false that all dependable knowledge is inductive; for the method of mathematics is not properly so described. The correct principle here is that all things that are of one basic logical class should be investigated by one method. Now concrete things and mathematical patterns are not of one logical type, hence the difference between the inductive method of the one and the deductive method of the other. Metaphysics studies a third logical class of entities, the universal categories of all actual and conceivable worlds. Physics studies this actual world; mathematics studies patterns each of which represents a feature of certain possible worlds (including perhaps the actual one—the mathematician does not care as to that) ; the metaphysician studies the most utterly basic features of experience and thought which are presupposed by any world whatever and by any truth whatever. This is logically a different type of question from either of the other two, and it calls for a different method.

What is this method? Here we find another apparent ground for the distrust of metaphysics. All reasoning is supposed to be either inductive or merely deductive. If it is deductive, then either it derives consequences from indubitable premises, or its results are purely hypothetical. But these are not exhaustive divisions. Metaphysics is not a deduction of consequences either from axioms dogmatically proclaimed true nor yet from mere arbitrary postulates or hypotheses. It is an attempt to describe the most general aspects of experience, to abstract from all that is special in our awareness, and to report as clearly and accurately as possible upon the residuum. In this process deduction from defined premises plays a role, but not the role of expanding the implications of axioms. The great historical error was to suppose that some metaphysical propositions have only to be announced to be seen true, and hence all their implications must be beyond questioning. The true role of deduction in metaphysics is not to bring out the content of the initially certain, but to bring out the meaning of tentative descriptions of the metaphysically ultimate in experience so that we shall be better able to judge if they do genuinely describe this ultimate. Axioms are not accepted as self-evident, then used to elicit consequences that must not be doubted. They are rather set up as *questions* whose full meanings only deduction of the consequences of possible answers can tell us.

When we know the meaning of the possible answers, we may, if we are lucky, be able to see that one of them is evidently true to that residuum of experience which is left when all details variable in imagination have been set aside. Thus, self-evidence or axiomatic status is the goal of the inquiry, not its starting point. Metaphysical deduction justifies its premises by the descriptive adequacy of its conclusions; it does not prove the conclusions by assuming the premises. In this, metaphysics is like inductive science. The difference is that "verification" in metaphysics is not through details but through what is left when all details are treated as indifferent. Metaphysics is not quantitative, because quantities are details of the world. Even the most general quantitative constants are details, with reference to all time and all space, and with reference to all possible worlds.

The relation of metaphysics to God is not hard to see. For (as nearly all theologians have conceived him) God is no detail of existence, but is precisely the individual whose individuality must be expressed in any possible world (which could only be a possible product of his creative power). The everlasting, omnipresent, ungenerated individual is either an absurdity, or he must be exhibited by the metaphysical residuum which survives the elimination of detail. God is the only individual whose essential individuality is as general as any universal; he is the one universal individual. (It can, I think, be shown that this involves no fatal paradox.) If metaphysics knows anything, it must either know God, or know that the idea of God is meaningless. Neutrality as to God means no metaphysics. The choice is a theistic metaphysics, or an atheistic metaphysics or a positivistic rejection of both God and metaphysics. This choice is not an easy one. Only the future can resolve it to the general satisfaction of thinking minds.

CHAPTER ELEVEN

THE LIMITATIONS OF
RELIGIOUS HUMANISM

WHAT IS THE ISSUE between theistic religion and religion without God, or "humanism"? For theistic religion the life more abundant consists in love for God and love for man in inseparable unity. For humanism the "law and the prophets" are summed up in love for man alone. But the issue is not really so simple. For humanism is concerned with man's control over nature, and it knows (or at least, some humanists know) that this control is not the result of hatred or indifference toward nature but of love in some sense. This love, which is not for man in particular, but for the universe, has been called "natural piety." Between love of the universe and love of a divine person there may seem to be little connection but only to a superficial view. The order and beauty of the creation have always been regarded by theists as the immanent rationality and goodness of God. And on the other side, if there is no universal mind in the cosmos, it has proved beyond the power of philosophy to state wherein the cosmic order consists. As Russell and Santayana and many others have admitted, the theoretical foundation of the scientist's trust in the reliability of discoverable natural uniformities is not apparent—apart, that is, from the theistic foundation that these men reject. Science is the "intellectual love" of, that is in lowest terms, trust in and admiration for, the cosmic whole regarded as an integrated system, and not as a mere aggregate of miscellaneous events. Religion can be viewed as the same attitude with a difference of emphasis and explicitness, rather than of implicit assumption. To say nature is worthy of being loved and to say there is a God are perhaps not ultimately distinguishable assertions. For what is God but that in or "behind" the cosmos which renders it worthy of trust and love?

The difference of emphasis spoken of is found, of course, in this, that to religion the cosmic unity is worthy not only of "intellectual love," but of devotion expressing the entire man in his intellectual, esthetic, and ethical aspects. It is involved in this completeness of devotion that to religion God is lovable because he himself loves, and that in a preëminently perfect way. Here is where humanism makes its best case. For, while science pictures nature in terms of rational order, it does not seem to indicate or presuppose any cosmic tenderness toward individuals, or any purpose to which their welfare is especially relevant. The falling rock reliably pursues its lawful course whether below it are only other rocks or complex organisms— a deer, a man—upon which its impact will inflict suffering or destruction. This simple consideration may well give pause to anyone contemplating the transition from the merely intellectual to the complete or religious love of nature.

Yet the transition is neither easily avoided (if one inquires deeply) nor necessarily invalidated by the objection mentioned. It is not easily avoided; for if order is not intelligible apart from reason, neither is reason intelligible apart from purpose, and purpose in turn is not to be divested of a social aspect which is love. Or, from another point of view, what an intellectual person loves with all his intellectual soul he loves also as a man; for the mind is a unity. The lives of scientists give some confirmation to this assertion. They have generally been persons whose love of nature has included a quite explicitly theistic aspect. And I suggest that it is in the main true that those who lack a philosophical perspective which exhibits a supreme lovableness in nature (such as is difficult if not impossible to conceive apart from theism) are also those who fail to add much to our undertanding of nature. Dewey and Russell and Santayana are, to my mind, typical in this regard. They have helped us to understand man, because they care about man; but nature at large they are but mildly interested in, and we owe no substantial illumination to them concerning it.

As for the falling rock, it is proof of the indifference of

nature (or the supreme power) only if it is clear that more good could be done to individuals *in general* by deviations from an orderly course of events than by the maintenance of such a course. And this is by no means clear. We can readily see that miracles could be indulged in by the cosmic power only at the price of diminishing the general reliability or predictability of nature, and perhaps its intellectual beauty; hence, we can hardly be sure that it would really be beneficial on the whole for falling rocks to be stopped in their tracks whenever some valuable organisms happened to be in their path. It is, indeed, obvious that part of the value of existence to organisms is that they are partly on their own, required to exercise their own foresight and powers of prevention.

It is not quite correct to say that the foregoing makes divine and human righteousness totally incomparable; that, whereas we feel a duty to be merciful, deity is free to be cruel or indifferent. The engineer has a duty to start the train about on time, although he may know that some individual is thereby doomed to bitter tears because the train leaves without him. The trains of nature perhaps cannot be permitted to forget their schedules—not because individuals do not matter, but precisely because individuals do matter, and because they cannot well exist if there are no schedules which are faithfully observed.

But although the arguments of humanism can perhaps be answered, its present position is rather strategic. For one thing, the traditional concepts of omnipotence, omniscience, and eternity have been shown to contain ambiguities and contradictions which philosophically equipped theists are only in our time learning to remove (see writings such as those of Whitehead, Calhoun, Garvie, Montague, Hocking). This work has not been so well publicized as that of Einstein, Heisenberg, or Darwin; yet it is no less epoch-making. How many know, for example, that most of the more brilliant non-Roman philosophical theologians do not now ascribe absolute foreknowledge (or timeless knowledge of all time) to deity? Or that this is not held to mean the renunciation of knowledge of all reality ("omniscience") but only a more exact definition of the meaning of "knowledge of all"?

Apart from this instance of cultural lag, there is the effect of the entanglement of institutional religion with economic arrangements which are now under criticism. Here, too, the humanistic arguments are somewhat more facile than cogent. The belief in a perfect, superhuman standard of goodness not only does not imply, but is incompatible with, the absolutizing of human institutions and codes, even ecclesiastical. Also, the true conception of a Supreme Being not only does not involve but helps to discredit notions of class superiority. Compared to the love which holds the universe together, the finest human understanding is vanishingly feeble and narrow, and the noblest human will is blind, brutal, and inconstant; and in this comparison, human equality is radically established.

Looking to the long future, it appears that there may always be temperaments inclined to humanism. It will always be simpler to fall back, for our basic relation to nature, upon unanalyzed "animal faith" than to humanize this instinctive trust through reflective theology. There is both justice and irony in giving to this simpler position the name of humanism. For it is only man's relation to man and to the subhuman which in this position is humanized, brought to a reflective level, while man's relation to what is above him remains in principle merely animal, a blind trust.

How far is it possible effectively to humanize human relations while consigning the cosmic relation to instinct? That is, how well can we love men without consciously loving the cosmic reality as God? It must be said that recent atheistic social philosophies have shown some tendency to condone, in the political order, the blind indifference to individuals which they posit of the universe at large.[1] Perhaps it is not possible to serve love with undivided mind while believing that nature is founded upon principles or powers which have no similarity to love.

There is at least this to be said for humanism, however. It has often been an effective protest against intellectual dishonesty and laziness in religion, as well as against the notion

---

1. The weaknesses of many non theistic social and political doctrines are penetratingly discussed in E. Heimann's *Freedom and Order* (1947).

that love of God can really be actualized apart from love of our human fellows. We may learn from the humanists to be more sensitive to the absurdity of a piety which falls short of simple decency and helpfulness in ordinary affairs, or even of bare honesty. (Think of pious parents who answer children's earnest and guileless questions with "well-meaning" lies, of pious teachers and scholars who manipulate history and philosophy to the greater glory of their supposedly infallible doctrines or institutions.) We may learn to realize more constantly and fully that loyalty to the objective God, whatever else it may be, must at least be devotion to the knowable truth, and to the full good of humanity.

CHAPTER TWELVE

DEWEY'S TREATMENT OF THEISM

T HE MOST INFLUENTIAL philosopher in this country is probably still John Dewey. Since his views seem rather remote from those expounded in this book, it seems in order to include a discussion of some of the differences. The weakness I find in Dewey's methodological practice is that he does not usually combine adequacy with the maximum sharpness. I shall illustrate. The great and, I feel confident, the valid contention of Dewey in religion is that a God conceived as in all respects perfect, complete and actual, a sheer identity of value sought and value achieved, makes all effort to achieve ideals meaningless, and is itself a meaningless pseudo-idea. To turn the ideal into the real, without qualification, in forming the idea of God is to substitute the existence of all good for the aspiration toward a good that might exist, and thus makes deity not the inspiration of human action but, as definitely as any atheistic universe, its repudiation or nullification. So much Dewey makes sharply clear, just short of that degree of sharpness that would tell us what the exact alternative to the error in question would be.

The error is the idea of a being in all respects "perfect," hence, unchangeable, unenrichable, indifferent ("impassible") to all loss or gain or results of striving. The alternative is, it is as clear as arithmetic, not the denial that there is a being truly perfect, but only the denial that there is a being *in all respects* perfect (meaning by the "perfect" an absolute maximum of value). For a being in some respects (say in accuracy of knowledge) perfect, but in some respects capable of increase in value (say in satisfaction, happiness) would not imply the irrelevance of human striving or of change. Human achievements in knowledge would then indeed not increase the accuracy of God's knowledge of the real, but by adding new content, new objects, for him to know accurately (for our knowledge itself would be known by him) they might increase the variety, richness, beauty, of the divine experience and so the divine happiness. Thus, God could literally be "served."

Although it is only rather recently that theologians and philosophers[1] have begun to consider such an idea of God as a being absolutely perfect in some respects only, there is excellent reason for thinking that religion has all along been concerned implicitly with this idea. God is perfect in power, knowledge, love, but is he perfect once for all in happiness? It may seem that absolute power, knowledge, and love are sufficient conditions of complete happiness. But this is so *only* if happiness is entirely independent of the nature of the things known, controlled, loved, *or* if the things are completely without power of self-determination. The first supposition is contradicted by experience; the second is the absolute denial of religion as the view that man is the image of God, endowed with some spark of creative power and initiative. It follows that perfect (that is, such that "none greater is conceivable") knowledge and power cannot mean such as would make the knower and active agent in every sense independent of the known and acted upon. We must give up perfection entirely, or admit that God is not in all respects beyond dependence and the possibility of gain.

It is not chiefly Dewey's fault that he did not find himself led to discuss a doctrine that theologians have so tardily condescended even to consider, although it is certainly time for his followers at least to realize that it is not "scientific method" to view as settled an issue involving three possible solutions, when but two of the three have been clearly stated and confronted with the evidence. Dewey, like multitudes of theologians, lumps together all notions of divine perfection, whether total

---

1. An excellent example is Dewey's colleague at Columbia, W. P. Montague, whose form of theism (or anything like it), Dewey has, so far as I can see, never honored with even a word of definite comment. See *The Ways of Things* (1940), pp. 110 ff., 511-40, for Montague's doctrine.

or qualified, and by his neglect of such sun-clear, formal considerations as "all," "some" and "none" (as to respects of perfection) leaves the theistic question from the rational point of view quite undecided. In such neglect, often found in his philosophizing, of the formally definite, Dewey seems indeed akin to and perhaps under the influence of his early master, Hegel, as well as, to some extent, James, rather than such thinkers as Leibniz and Peirce, who to a greater extent knew how to combine precision with comprehensiveness.

An issue much discussed in connection with Dewey's philosophy is that of the relations of the human self or person to the physical world at large. Dewey complains of misunderstanding here. It does not seem to me that he has attained the definiteness which the problem admits of. Granted the behavioristic account of the self, in the moderate form given this account by Dewey, the following question remains: Is the awareness of an other, a not-oneself, essentially and *always,* or accidentally and *sometimes,* what we call "social," in some way or degree sympathetic (rather than merely exploitative), however little conscious or however rudimentary this sympathy may sometimes be? This is the basic issue separating Dewey from the only comparably adequate thinkers of our time, Bergson and Whitehead.

The question, Is there a God? is the social question taken at its maximum; the question, Is an electron a bit of mere dead "matter"? is the social question at the opposite or minimal extreme. Does the cosmos as a whole have personal behavior (if one wishes to speak behavioristically) in a supreme fashion; does the electron have a rudimentary kind of sensitivity, memory and the like, behavioristically regarded? This seems to me the solid kernel in the idealism-realism controversy about the relations of mind and matter, and I seem to see Dewey talking almost all around it, but perhaps never really reaching it. His rejection of absolutistic conceptions of God is in harmony with the social view, for absolute-perfection-in-all-respects, whatever else it may be, is precisely non social, since it is non mutual in all its relations and cannot literally sympathize with or care for anything. The "pluralism" Dewey calls for is not opposed to theism, but only to pseudo-theism. Perfect love tolerates really active other individuals, permitting them to react upon it, for such action and reaction is love in the generic sense—of which hatred is only a special case or perversion.

Dewey comes very close to admitting God as the supreme social other. He speaks (as Schaub points out) of that "enveloping whole" by which, in genuine religious experience, we are "sustained and expanded," and in the presence of which "we put off mortality and live in the universal," and thereby enjoy "peace in action, not after it." Religion has no quarrel with these statements of Dewey, nor with a pluralism which can yet admit that there is an in some sense inclusive being. At this point I see nothing but vagueness between Dewey and the more definite view of religious theism.

We owe to Dewey at least two things: the resolute and patient thinking for himself on a grand scale over many fields; and the exhibition of a remarkable sense for social relations, for what I take to be important elements in Christian love, such as many a Christian has lacked. This sense has clarified theoretical as well as practical problems, and only needs developing to go the whole way to an adequate philosophy. But one direction in which development is needed is toward greater use of formal clarity, mathematical explicitness, which is after all social, since it is the only way of achieving exact communication of ideas. A curious example of Dewey's tendency to avoid fully definite generalizations is noted by Savery. What is Dewey's answer to the fact of death as an apparent nullification of human efforts? His answer might be, the immortality of the race. But *is* the race immortal? Where has Dewey even mentioned this simple question? The other answer, if one does not admit personal immortality, might be that the "enveloping whole" will continue, even after the possible destruction of man by some planetary catastrophe, to treasure the sum of human enjoyments as actually having occurred, and to create within itself other forms of significant life.

Dewey leaves everything much vaguer than that, though to some this seems the minimum of religious background capable of sustaining action in the face of realistic reflection. Yet, he may have been wise. His generation could hardly, as a whole, have found its way through the maze of problems created by dogmatic distortions of religion, which only now can be ignored in favor of the more direct statements of the content of religious thought and feeling which have become available. This greater freedom to be positive and definite in religion without sacrifice of "intelligence" is in no small measure Dewey's gift to us all.

CHAPTER THIRTEEN

RUSSELL ON ETHICS
AND RELIGION

PERHAPS THE MOST PENETRATING skeptical intellect
of recent times is the great logician Bertrand Russell. What
significance shall we attach to his skepticism?

In an essay called "My Mental Development,"[1] Bertrand
Russell gives us real help in understanding his basic motives and
values. His grandmother, by whom he was largely brought up,
"had the Protestant belief in private judgment and the supremacy of the individual conscience" and nurtured him on such
texts as "Thou shalt not follow a multitude to do evil" and "Be
strong, and of a good courage . . . for the Lord thy God is with
thee whithersoever thou goest." His parents, who died when he
was a very small child, were freethinkers, with ardent reformist
tendencies derived from Mill. In a campaign for political office,
his father, who had semi-privately remarked that the question of
birth control should be referred to the medical profession, was
accused of advocating infanticide and called a "filthy foul-
mouthed rake." Russell's acrid comment—"The student of comparative sociology may be interested in the similarities between
rural England in 1868 and urban New York in 1940" (referring
to the abuse heaped upon Russell himself at that time)—is not,
one fears, wholly unjustified, even though there are some
differences between the two cases. At the age of twenty-one,
when Russell first came to know "the main outlines of my
parents' lives and opinions," he had himself already broken

1. In *The Philosophy of Bertrand Russell*. Ed., P. A. Schilpp. Evanston and
Chicago: Northwestern University, 1944. Pp. 5-8. References in the present chapter are to this volume.

away from religious beliefs. However, to learn that his parents had preceded him in agnosticism and in the liberal political opinions which he had nourished through readings in his grandfather's library must have come as confirmation and encouragement. It is also not surprising that a boy whose passion was mathematics and to whom religion had not, it seems, been presented by anyone of great intellectual power should have convinced himself that the arguments for religious doctrines are unsound. Is not one of the deepest causes of philosophical disagreement that some men in their early days encounter exceptional intellectual power chiefly in a religious, others chiefly in a nonreligious, form? The effects of this difference, I am persuaded, are often lifelong.

Russell says he renounced belief in a First Cause upon reading Mill's remark: "My father taught me that the question, 'Who made me?' cannot be answered, since it immediately suggests the further question, 'Who made God?' " Yet all that follows from the elder Mill's contention is that the argument for a supreme cause cannot use as its major premise the statement that everything has a cause. But this never was the premise of the argument, but rather that everything whose nonexistence is possible (as shown by its not having always existed, or in come other way) depends for its existence upon something whose nonexistence is impossible, or again, that everything which exists through another involves something which exists through itself. That whose nature is separable from existence requires a cause to render possible the union of this nature with existence; but that whose nature it is to exist requires no cause for the possibility of its existence (it being, just in itself, the cause, not of its possible, but of its necessary, existence). Now it is true that the distinction between self-existence and existence through another—necessary and contingent existence—lacks the seeming obviousness of the ordinary idea of cause, so that what the young Russell was encountering was the subtlety of the theological problem. This subtlety might have attracted, rather than repelled, him had he known those able to do justice to it. Unfortunately, the classical treatments of this matter are crude and indeed, in my opinion, as in that of most modern philosophers, quite untenable.

We must note another difficulty with religion as Russell saw and sees it. During the first World War, he says, "The War Office sent for me and exhorted me to preserve a sense of humor. With great difficulty I refrained from saying that the casualty lists made me split my sides with laughter. No, I will not be serene and above the battle; what is horrible I will see as horrible, and not as part of some blandly beneficent whole."[2] For my part, not only do I feel this reaction to be humanly noble, I think it is also, though unwittingly, theologically sound. And I suspect with Russell that the attitude he is opposing is to be associated with "limited sympathies and a secure income." The traditional view of God as purely "impassive" and serene while men endure agonies on earth (if not in hell besides) makes God less even than a Bertrand Russell, makes limitation of sympathy carried to the absolute degree a divine attribute, with the implication that we should try to be likewise. Many of us have come to reject this view. There is no "blandly beneficent whole," either of or beyond the world, but rather, as Whitehead and Berdyaev and Niebuhr teach, a divine who takes into himself the tragedy of the world and whose joy in his creation is a tragic joy.

But why cannot or does not God prevent the tragedy? Russell, apropos of Leibniz, says: "Evil . . . *may* have been necessary in order to produce a greater good." However, he adds: "the good *may* have been necessary in order to produce a greater evil. If a world which is partly bad may have been created by a wholly benevolent God, a world which is partly good may have been created by a wholly malevolent Devil. . . . . One is as likely as the other." Only "optimistic bias," Russell thinks, has led to the neglect of the second or "unpleasant" possibility.[3]

Here I think Russell himself exhibits bias and a certain resultant lack of adequate analysis. First, a wholly malevolent devil is a pseudo-concept void of coherent meaning. No will can be bent wholly on evil done to others; for, without some element of sympathetic identification with others, one cannot even know that they exist as sentient beings. Sympathy, not

2. P. 725.
3. P. 727.

hate or indifference, is the positive and expansive factor in social awareness and is in some degree presupposed by the negative factors. Moreover, cruelty springs from weakness, fear, envy, and other attitudes possible only to beings which are not cosmic in scope and power. The cosmos could not be held together and ordered by malevolence, which, as Plato argued, is always partly divided against itself and is also incapable of an objective grasp of reality; but the cosmos could be held together by an all-sympathetic co-ordinator, a shepherd of all beings. In the second place, the theistic alternative to a devilish coordinator (or no coordinator) need not be the orthodox conception of a wholly absolute and blandly serene world dictator. I refer, not to the idea that God may be imperfect either in good will or in power, but to the possibility that perfection of power is quite other than the capacity for absolute coercion or dictation. Russell's oversight here, I suggest, is that he has never understood how freedom is the core of individuality. The tragedy of existence may be due to the truth that value lies in spontaneous experiences, individual acts of feeling and thought, which, as such, *could* not be completely determined by any other individual or any antecedent conditions. God does not arrange the details of the world with a view to the exact amount of evil required for the greater good; he only subjects the self-arranging of necessarily partly free acts to a guiding influence whose principle is not the right mixture of good and evil but the right mixture of freedom and constraint. There is no such mixture which would guarantee the elimination of evil; for if there is *any* freedom in a multiplicity of beings, there is potentiality of discord between them, a potentiality the total nonrealization of which is infinitely unlikely. On the other hand, if there were no freedom, there would be neither good nor evil. Thus, the right mixture of freedom and constraint is not one which would eliminate the risks of evil (and, thereby, also all opportunities for good) but rather one which provides the maximal surplus of opportunities over risks. This optimal balance of opportunity over risk may well be at a high, not a low, level of risk. The risks in a mouse's life are trivial compared to those in a man's and so are the opportunities. This seems to express a law of value. Hence, the evil in the world does not necessarily mean either nonbenevolence or imperfection of power in God, for perfection of power is power to set the opportunity-risk relation at the optimal point. In view of the evil that nevertheless results, the divine satisfaction in the world is not "bland" but tinged with vicarious suffering, like that of Bertrand Russell surveying human tragedies.

Professor Brightman makes a valiant attempt, whose "truly Christian forbearance" is justly appreciated by Russell, to point out to the famous philosopher that the possibilities for religious theory are not exhausted by orthodoxy and atheism. Russell, in fact, has nowhere done any justice to the view of God as neither simply infinite, absolute, independent nor simply finite, relative, and dependent, but rather with each of these sets of attributes in different aspects of his being. In his reply, Russell fails to make good this neglect and maintains only that he prefers the arguments for God's existence in the older systems because at least they are definite (even though fallacious), whereas the newer systems, according to our illustrious writer, lack anything that can even pretend to be a proof. But while it may be true that the new form of natural theology has not (or until recently had not) developed formal proofs comparable in definiteness to the old, this is perhaps a temporary defect. And it might turn out that the fallacies in the older proofs were largely due to the attempt to justify an erroneous conception of God, in which case their failure is itself a partial argument for the true conception. The "finite-infinite" God (Brightman) is a more complex and subtle conception (reminding one, in this respect, of the particle-wave concept of physics) than that of the merely infinite God, and so proofs for it might have to be more complex and subtle. But they might, for all that, be just as definite, and in addition they might be sound. The truth often is a bit complex and subtle. The older theologies were elaborated by men comparable in intellectual power to Russell. Only as the newer view is elaborated by men of similar caliber (such as Whitehead), can we learn whether or not it can meet the criticisms of leading skeptics. Unfortunately, the latter, including Russell, rather ignore Whitehead than criticize him.

I wish to suggest one argument which can be defended

against the classical objections. The world is an ordered whole, at least to the extent that multitudes of beings coexist, that is to say, form tolerable environments for one another. There is frustration and conflict, but *mainly* things agree with and support one another. This vast mutual sustaining and cooperating of things either is due to myriads of causal agents, none sufficiently powerful to order the rest to each other, or is due to the control of the many agents by a single radically superior agent, setting limits to the rest and influencing all in the direction of harmony and some over-all design. Now the axiom here is that plurality of agents amounts, in the absence of a supreme agent, to chaos. ("Too many cooks spoil the broth," is an inadequate, but suggestive, indication of the principle.) From this axiom it clearly does not follow that the supreme agent will require a further agent to order itself to the lesser agents. The supreme agent will relate all to itself and itself to all. In this will be its supremacy. The cosmic agent, however, would not in every respect be infinite or absolute. To impose the cosmic order it does not have to determine absolutely the action of lesser agents. For the cosmic order is not absolute. Things do conflict and frustrate one another and only *in the main* are mutually harmonious. Therefore, the ground of this harmony need not possess absolute power of determination; but it must possess absolute power to set *limits* to the in-principle chaotic self-determinations of lesser agents. I cannot follow further here either the presuppositions or the conclusion of the argument for a finite-infinite God outlined in this paragraph.

Russell's inability to see any theoretical basis for theology is combined with an inability—less palatable to some of his fellow skeptics—to see any theoretical basis for ethics.[4] He proposes a strict dualism between scientific judgments of fact and necessarily nonscientific judgments of value. This dualism—which is deplored, but not, I think, decisively refuted, by Lindeman and Buchler—might also be stated as that of means versus ends. The solution may lie in a more radical interpretation of this distinction. The only end that is absolutely such is the

---

4. Pp. 719-24, 728.

maximizing of the value-content of the universe. Assuming that
the cosmos has at any given time a total value-content and
assuming a principle which measures increase in this content,
then it may be that science is competent to determine in detail the applications of the principle to fact, except—and it is
a large exception—to the extent that imponderables of feeling
and circumstance compel us to act upon intuitive hunches.
But the basic *principle* of cosmic value-increase is purely
metaphysical and theological. People often apply the principle
without explicating it; Russell realizes what is involved in
denying, or attempting to deny, it. Or, at least, he almost
realizes it—for fully to realize it is, if I mistake not, to see that
the denial is not genuinely conceivable. According to Russell,
to say a desire is right is only to say that one desires that others
should have the desire. Russell admits that this does not entirely
satisfy his own feeling that some desires are really good and
some not. For example, he does not know how to refute by any
rational argument the, to him, detestable view that "good"
is essentially "good for some master-race or class," to which
other men are to serve merely as means.

Now here, as in the theological question (really the same
question), it seems that Russell fails to see all the possibilities.
"Good for all men" is not logically preferable to "good for
some men" *if*, in either case, only human factors are considered; but this is because there is in purely human terms no
logic, no rationale, of good at all. How can bits of happiness
in several men, whether all mankind or only a class of men,
be added together to make one good? The good is satisfaction,
but there is no man whose satisfaction contains and sums up
human satisfactions. Each man has only his own happiness.
Nay, he does not have even that, for happiness as an ideal
refers to the general course of life over years, and no one ever
enjoys any happiness but that of a given moment. What is
needed for a logic of good is some conception of how values
can contribute to an inclusive value or satisfaction. Given that
conception, then to maintain that the satisfactions of the master-race form a total not in any way increased by adding also
those enjoyed by other men is to speak illogically. We can
argue in esthetic terms that whatever it be that puts together

the various value-experiences in a super-experience must, on known esthetic laws, derive depth and intensity from the contrasts between different types of included experiences, both of men and of other sentient beings. But what can such a super-experience be, if not the divine experience? The end is not just the good for me, the good for my class, or even for all mankind; the end is the good for me, the good for mankind, the good for all sentient beings as, *ipso facto,* also good for the one being which measures good and evil, because to it all hearts are open, whose service really is freedom because it is precisely *our* joy in free action that, poured into the sympathetic experience of deity, constitutes our contribution to the divine joy, just as our avoidance of suffering for ourselves spares God the tragic participation in that suffering which his unlimited sympathy would involve, should the suffering occur.

It is true that one must still find the connection between our own desire or approval and the divine self-realization. To say, "divine self-realization is good," is at least to express our approval of it. But it can, I believe, be shown that he who faces reality cannot withhold such approval; that no lesser or different objective can withstand rational criticism, so that no other is philosophically defensible.

The difficulties of Russell's skepticism appear also in his discussion of social and political issues.[5] Thus, to Professor Bode's contention that the English philosopher's educational views rest upon a false contrast between the individual and the community or between the man and the citizen, Russell replies, in part, that there is a conflict between the demands of world citizenship (which should be given priority) and less inclusive associations. But he also seems to hold that the individual is more than the citizen, even the world citizen, whereas Bode's view is that God himself (were the concept allowable) would have to behave as a citizen of the cosmos. Bode holds, too, that the notion of an individual as more or less independent of citizenship is partly a result of the illegitimate theological notion of absolute self-sufficiency.

Here, once more, there is a neglected alternative. If world

---

5. pp. 731 ff.

citizenship must have priority over local citizenship, by the same principle the ultimate value (as the Stoics held) is cosmic citizenship. But if we suppose, as Russell feels driven to do, that the cosmos apart from this planet may be inanimate and unconscious, then cosmic citizenship must appear to us a concept of doubtful meaning. Further, unless the cosmic community is conceived as united in a divine experience, the contrast between citizen and individual cannot, in spite of Bode, be overcome, and the attempt to overcome it leads, as Russell says, to tyranny and the loss of intimate personal values. But if we understand the universal society to contain one ideally social being, and this means not a being in every respect absolute or self-sufficient but one whose social appreciations are wholly adequate and unstinted (and who, in this unique sense is indeed a citizen), then we can carry through the insight that the individual just is a term of social relations and also do justice to the fact that there are in every man values which do not fully express themselves in his relations to other men—values of individual feeling and awareness of nature and God, never wholly accounted for in communications to others—still less in any political arrangements. But such values are all communicated to God, and in the dim depths of awareness we enjoy this fact from which arises our sense that we and all our values are just that much added to the whole.

It should be a matter of note to those interested in religion that antitheistic philosophers seem unable to escape from such unlivable doctrines as that the man is only the citizen or, at the opposite extreme, that the man is an individual whose connection with the universal social good is without rational principle.

CHAPTER FOURTEEN

RELIGIOUS BEARINGS OF
WHITEHEAD'S PHILOSOPHY

So OLD and widely used a term as "God," it is frequently said, should not be given a radically new meaning. Perhaps this is just; but it should be remembered that there are several ancient meanings for "God" rather than but one. Admitting that the God of some present-day philosophers is not the God of the Scholastics or of Calvin, it does not automatically follow that the new view is in hopeless disagreement with that of Jesus and the prophets. For who (unless the Pope) guarantees that the older theologians were in agreement with the founder of the religion they sought to interpret? "Jesus above the heads of his disciples" may be applied to theological disciples as well as to less intellectual ones. The Scholastics and Calvin derive from many sources besides the biblical—for example, Greek philosophy and Roman law. Perhaps the new view of God is really, in some respects at least, a return to the Gospel conception.

Among those accused of misusing the divine name, Whitehead is prominent. The accusation has just been made again, this time with more careful documentation than usual.[1] Now, admittedly, Whitehead has set his statements about God in a highly complex intellectual context. Nor is his exposition always all that could be desired. For these reasons his idea of God cannot without difficulty be taken over by religious persons. Much more than this has not, I think, been established

---

1. S. L. Ely, *The Religious Availability of Whitehead's God*. Madison, Wisconsin: University of Wisconsin Press, 1942. Ely's tragically premature death occurred some time after this paragraph was first published.

against its religious availability. Men can, indeed, as Professor Ely remarks, have God on much simpler terms from religious resources. On the other hand, religious persons need not be obscurantists, they need not be without interest in the rational unity of culture, including religion, science, and art, and Whitehead's effort in this direction is, in the opinion of many, one of the most momentous ever undertaken. Further, it could, I think, be shown that certain religious values enshrined in Whitehead's doctrine have often been neglected in religious practice partly because the climate of philosophical and theological opinion was hostile to them. Never before, I believe, has a really first-rate philosophical system so completely and directly as Whitehead's supported the idea that there is a supreme love which is also the Supreme Being. Such a philosophy may help to bring practice more into accord than in the past with the ethical principle that the general good, the good we all seek in proportion as we love all creatures, is the only aim that can stand rational criticism.

The evaluation of Whitehead's contribution to religious thought has been impeded by the widespread use of equivocal terms in our theological tradition. Through this equivocation doctrines acquire credit which is not really due them. Whitehead is trying to be intellectually honest and clear. This forces him to break with traditional terminology at some points, and those who have not been accustomed to judge that terminology by rigorous standards may infer that Whitehead is sacrificing the religious values supposed to be enshrined in the terminology. For instance, he is sometimes accused of offering an "impersonal principle" in place of a "personal God," all the more so because in his earliest discussions of this topic he did speak of deity as a "principle of concretion," and indeed it seems doubtful if prior to the time of *Process and Reality* the philosopher had thought out in his own mind the great conception of divinity embodied in that book. But actually, what Whitehead is saying there comes closer to the religious feeling of the divine as personal than does Augustinianism or Thomism, if these are held to the logical implications of their axioms.

What is an individual, a person? A person involves a character, a complex of personality traits (including bodily traits) which are embodied in successive acts or experiences. These acts "express" the character, but are not identical with or included in it. If they were thus identical or included, a wise man would have a different wisdom, or become foolish, every time his experience changed, that is, every time the temperature altered, or with every new sentence as he reads a book. The function of terms like "character" is to point to a contrast between the at least relatively permanent and the variable in the man. True, a man may act "out of character," and in this sense character, in such as we are, is not wholly fixed or definite. But still, not every change is change in character. John Jones remains "himself," when he looks out of the window whether he sees rain, snow, or neither. If it were otherwise, "John Jones" would never refer to anybody until the man was dead. For only with death do changes in a man's experiences and acts come to an end. But the function of proper names surely is not limited to their use in writing the biography of the deceased! If we know *who* John Jones is while he lives, although obviously we know none of the precise changes he may suffer in future experience, it follows that personal indentity is something to which numerous particular changes of experience and action are neutral. This is the very freedom of a man, that he is not committed, by the personal identity which emerged as his embryo became a human self, nor by any later phase of his growth, to any determinate future acts. Each such act will be self-decided, to a certain extent, when it takes place; limited in possibilities, of course, by the character already laid down, but not for all that narrowed down to a single possibility for the given moment and circumstances.

In orthodox theology there occurred the colossal equivocation of maintaining:

1) God's action of willing simply *is* his character ("essence")

2) This action is free (he creates this world, but might have created a different one, or none)

Since the essence, or self-identity, of a being is the only one *that* being could have, it follows that if the essence is the willing, no different willing was possible for that being. If then, on the assumptions, God willed to create this world, he could not but have so willed. I am persuaded, after considerable discussion of the matter with proponents of orthodox theory, that there is here sheer contradiction, or words with no meaning at all.

What does Whitehead do? He removes the contradiction, or equivocation, by denying (1), thus admitting a real distinction between the acts of volition and the character or essence of deity. The character is the "primordial nature," what God is eternally, simply in being himself. But the acts constitute part of the "consequent nature," the *de facto* experience, or concrete state of God, which *expresses* the eternal character, but does not constitute it. (That there is *some* such concrete consequent state belongs to the essence, but not which among possible such states.)

Again, take the following doctrine of orthodoxy:

1) God knows infallibly that a world containing men, etc., exists

2) Some other world might have existed (or no world) instead of this one (the world's existence is contingent)

3) God's knowing is his essence

From (3) it follows that the knowing could not but have been just what in fact it actually is. But according to (2) the world which God knows to exist might not have existed, in which case the knowledge that it exists (which according to (1) and (3) could not have failed to obtain) would have been false knowledge. Now what follows from a possibility is also possible. Yet (1) declares that the falsity of God's knowledge is impossible (the meaning of "infallibility"). So we have a flat contradiction. To say that God's knowledge would have been the same entity, had the world not existed, only it would have been knowledge that the world did not exist, rather than knowledge that it exists, is merely to repeat the contradiction in another form. For "God knows that the world exists" is incompatible with "the world does not exist," while "God knows that the world does *not* exist" is compatible with and implies "the world does not exist." But two propositions, the one compatible, the other incompatible, with the same third proposition, cannot affirm the same entity! The entity which would be the same in God whether the world is or is not can only be described as "God knows," but not as "he knows that the world exists," nor as "he knows that the world does not exist." So either such definite knowledge as to the status of the world is not in God, or something which could have been otherwise is in God. Indeterminate knowledge that "one of the two is true, the world exists, or the world does not exist,' is scarcely what anyone means by omniscience; but it is all that can, without sheer contradiction, be affirmed of God if his actuality is the same as his necessary essence.

Whitehead once more eliminates contradiction by denying that the essence of God is his total reality. Another world was indeed possible; but it would have meant another divine knowledge, which therefore must also have been possible. Another divine knowledge does not, however, mean another divine essence or character; for character determines only a certain generic quality or manner of knowing, not any actual knowing in its concreteness. This generic quality involves a unique excellence of knowing which we may call infallibility (Whitehead does not use the term, but he does say that the divine knowledge is perfect, and that it coincides with the truth). Whether God knows that there are men, or that there are not men (in case none exist), either way, he knows with certainty and exactitude, so that the world which he knows is just what he knows it to be. Infallibility, as a quality of all possible states of divine knowing, belongs to the primordial nature of deity, but any actual knowing to the consequent nature. Only the former is eternal and immutable; the latter is everlasting, imperishable and incorruptible in what it has already become, but perpetually "in flux," in the sense that new phases of the world process mean new states of divine knowing added to those previously achieved.

But, you ask, would not a perfect knowledge survey all phases of the world process at once, whether these phases be *for us* past, present, or future? The Whiteheadian answer is that terms like "universe," or "the whole of time," are "demonstrative pronouns" which get their meaning from their context, and a partly new meaning each moment. There is no "all" of events, eternally fixed and the same, but an ever-growing totality. Time, says Bergson—and Whitehead agrees—is creation or nothing. This means, the function of time is to settle one by one issues that eternity, or the uncreated, does not settle. The Thomistic doctrine that divine knowledge of our future acts is not of acts future to God's knowing, but, as it were, simultaneous with his eternity (since his knowing is not "before" or "after" but above time altogether) simply assumes that time has a settled character from the standpoint of eternity—which is the basic question at issue. The doctrine really deprives time or process of intelligible meaning. An event cannot be fully known beforehand; for it does not exist to be known until it happens. Much less can it be known eternally; for much less does it exist eternally. The famous Thomistic solution, thus, so far from alleviating the paradox of "foreknowledge," infinitely aggravates it. If I have not freedom to settle today what was unsettled eternally, or for an eternal knowledge, how could I have freedom to settle today what was unsettled yesterday? For what is settled eternally cannot have been unsettled yesterday or ever. So, as Bergson says, we are (on the assumption in question) merely "re-editing eternity," and time is superfluous or empty of meaning. But if our freedom is thus illusory, then whence our very idea of freedom, even as applied to deity? To remove the paradox, we must say that eternity is merely the neutral noncommittal background common to all times, leaving all details unsettled so that they may be settled (and the settlement known) when and as process actualizes such details. "What will be will be"— yes, but there is nothing in *particular* that will be; there are only certain more or less general limitations imposed upon the future from the standpoint, not of eternity, but of each present, with its partly novel "determining tendencies" for what may come after it. What will-be will be—and also, what may-or-may-not-be may or may not be—but the more we approach the "standpoint of eternity," the more do the definite will-be's give place to mere may-be's.

Many philosophers besides Bergson and Whitehead have taken the foregoing position, and not a few (*e.g.,* Socinus and Fechner) have applied it to theology. Whitehead is merely the most elaborate and incisive and thorough of these; the most thorough in that he has more completely thought out the implications of the idea of time as not simply something created, but as the order of the creating itself, the way in which the uncreated or indeterminate is related to the created or determined. The result is that Whitehead has, not a less but a more, "personal" deity than Augustine or Thomas, if personal means being an individual with a character expressible freely in acts of knowledge, choice, and love. God "shares with each creature its actual world"; he takes into his actuality, as "consequent" upon process, the life of the world, somewhat as we (in infinitely less adequate fashion) take into ourselves experiences of our friends. He does not plot it all out in eternity, and with a single moveless stare register the result. He lives, genuinely lives, in unison with our living, and the only moveless feature is the basic character of infallibility of knowing, perfection of love or cherishing, adequacy of eternal ideal or underlying purpose. Character in God, it is true, does not have to emerge, cannot improve or degenerate, and cannot in his acts be violated, but is fixed and binding so that never will or could he act out of character. But since being "in character" is the mere common denominator of all the acts, it cannot involve what is peculiar to any of them.

Not only does Whitehead accept the distinction between personality or essence, and experiences or acts, without which none of these ideas retains any meaning; he gives an intelligible analysis of the relation between the two sides of deity. Men have often distinguished verbally between God as he is "absolutely," or "in himself," and as he is relatively, or for us, or as "manifested" in the creation. But they have generally failed to endow the distinction with anything like a clear and consistent meaning. Worse, they have tended to suggest that God *qua* absolute, *or* as independent of the world, is superior to God as related to the world. But in that case, the existence of the world is sheer mistake. We face a trilemma: God alone or simply in himself is inferior, superior, or merely equal, to God-with-the-world. If inferior, then deity acquires value from the world process, he has a consequent nature which is in process of never-ending actualization, as Whitehead maintains. This is a forthright position. But if, on the contrary, God-alone is superior to God-with-the-world, God must degrade himself in creating. We are then by our very existence blots on the divine perfection. To maintain this is self-stultifying. If, finally, God-alone is merely equal to God-with-the-world, then the act of creation was futile as measured in terms of the divine being. (And what other measure can there be? Is not omniscience the measure of all truth and value? If the significance of the creation cannot be expressed in terms of the divine, there can be no such significance.) This position too is self-stultifying. A man cannot significantly deny all significance to his very existence.

How then is God-with-the-world superior to God-alone? Quite simply—as the concrete is superior to the abstract. In abstraction from all stages of the world-process (and the idea of deity alone, or as not related to the world, is just this abstraction) God—not simply for us, but for himself—is "abstract," "deficient in actuality." The merely eternal purpose in God is the source of value, but not the value itself. Actual value is not mere intent or cause of achievement, but achievement itself. All such achievement is an emergent, a creation, even if it be divine achievement. Not that deity existed first or eternally without any achievement; but that always, primordially and everlastingly, God has created and creates. The world process had no beginning (Whitehead does not explicitly discuss the point, but this seems the reasonable construction), so that always God was concrete, actual. However, actualization of personality, at least on this highest level, is an inexhaustible affair, since here potentiality is absolutely infinite. More is always possible, even for God; or especially for God, since our own capacity for growth, within the limits of a human personality, seems not unlimited.

"Why does not God once for all, eternally, actualize all possible values?" Answer: because there are incompatible goods; actualization is an art, and every beauty excludes others. The "beauty of all possible beauties" is not any actual beauty at all, but mere chaos. Tragedy lies not in conflict of good with mere evil (only fanatics imagine this) but of good with good. On this profound point, as on many, Whitehead and Berdyaev, quite independently, reach the same conclusion.

Creation is thus not a mere superfluous "condescension" of deity, but his very life. We are co-workers with God, in that we add nuances of feeling to the "ocean of feeling" which is the richness of his ever-growing experience. This will be parodied, but only parodied, by the charge that thus we men lose all religious humility and view ourselves as necessary to God, or as capable of effecting "improvement" or possible "corruption" of his character. All this is excluded by the doctrine of a primordial fixed character of deity. God will be *himself* whatever we do, and would have been had none of us ever existed. True, he would not have had the same experiences or the same concrete value. But the abstract character traits, such as infallibility, or lovingness ("tenderness," is one word used by Whitehead here), owe nothing, simply nothing, to us. This is the untouchable holiness of deity. The alternatives of divine action are never between fallible and infallible, or right and not right. They are alternatives as to particular content, but the generic form of infallibility and appropriateness of response to the content is everlastingly fixed.

The foregoing paragraph can be summed up in another way, by saying that for Whitehead God is still the "necessary" being, if that means that his existence is necessary, or that his essence, the perfection which distinguishes him as individual from all others, is inseparable from his existence, and is identical with that existence. But at the same time, Whitehead can agree with modern logic, and also with Existentialist philosophies, that the most concrete and complete form of reality, which he calls actuality, is never necessary, is always transcendent of essence or fixed nature. God's existence is his essence, but his actuality is infinitely more than his essence. This is not, I shall now show, a mere quibble.

The contrast, essence-existence, is derivative from a more basic duality, that of possibility-actuality. This is not the same pair of concepts. A dog who fears the brandished whip is concerned about a possible feeling of pain. The possibility may become actual. But suppose it does, will the sum of existents be thereby increased? The dog exists already. Shall we say, the pain does not but might exist? This is linguistically possible, but such usage slurs over a distinction that for some purposes is fundamental. The sense in which the dog exists, and the sense in which its pain exists are different in principle. The occurrence of the pain is an event; now it is somewhat unnatural, and as we shall see it is philosophically misleading, to say that events exist. On the one hand, we need the word "exist" for things or persons, for men, mountains, God. On the other hand, such existence of things or persons is not the strict alternative to essence or to possibility, and we also need a word for this alternative. Granted that the dog exists and will continue to exist for the next hour, let us say, this does not decide among various possibilities. It is possible he will be whipped, possible he will not be. His existence is common to these possibilities. The strict alternative to "possible" is "actual," in the sense of Whitehead's "actual entity," that is, a unit event or "occasion of experience." Such a unit event or unit experience is what it is, there is nothing else that "it" might be or have been (although some other event might have occurred in its stead). Thus, it is states, events, occurrences, or occasions that definitely decide among possibilities. Since we need to be able to say that dogs and men exist, and these entities are not strictly contrasted to possibilities, whereas events are thus contrasted, we had better not say that events exist, but rather that they occur, or are actual.

What exists is an individual thing or person; wherein then does the existence of such an individual consist? It consists, according to some contemporary logicians, including Whitehead, simply in this, that there are successive actual instances of a certain kind of event—for example, human experiences embodying the personality traits of John Jones, Jonesian experiences, as it were. But the mere existence of a specified individual leaves it undetermined just which instances of the kind of event in question are actual; thus, for example, "I" may exist tomorrow, either in a state of health or of sickness, that is, either through a series of actual experiences and acts expressive of health, or a series expressive of ill health, and either lying (or sitting) in bed, or "up and about"; that is, thanks to events with one or the other set of characters—in any case, however, I shall exist, provided there be some actual events embodying the personality traits characteristic of the events through which "I" have hitherto existed. (Included among "personality traits" is a tendency to remember some of the earlier portions of the series of experiences called "mine," and other types of relationship binding the various experiences into a single sequence. Now the ordinary individual is highly selective with respect to the events which can actualize it, and therefore its existence is uncertain; it makes peculiar demands upon the course of events, and these demands may not be fulfilled. Thus, existence in such cases is "contingent," like the actualities which may or may not occur to embody it. But suppose an individual whose personality traits would be expressed in any possible events—and it is arguable that the divine individual, God, may be defined in this manner—then this individual "exists" necessarily or by its very essence, not because there is here an exception to the law that an "actuality" or happening is always contingent and indemonstrable, but because the only possible alternative to an actuality embodying deity is—another actuality also embodying deity, so far as its personality traits or essential characters are concerned, though as different as you please in inessential qualities of the events.

All this is less difficult than may appear at first sight. Events, experiences, constituting a human personal history vary with changes in one small region of the world on the earth's surface—for example, with temperature changes. If the changes are too great, the personal history comes to an end. Instead of "my" experience of cold, if the temperature drops too low, there will be no human experience at all, just as there will be none of heat if the temperature rises too high. But it inheres in the idea of "God" that his existence cannot be contingent in this way. Whatever happens in the world, "omniscience," infallible or divine knowledge, is equally possible with respect to that world. No doubt, actually to know infallibly, that is divinely, that a certain world, W^1, exists is a different state of cognitive actuality from knowing infallibly that some other kind of world, W^2, exists instead. Omniscience, thus, is not a determinate actuality, but a property or essence which may be embodied in this or that possible actuality, and with respect to any world you please. Any actual omniscient awareness of a given world will be contingent. But it does not follow that the existence of the omniscient being or individual is contingent. For that existence is actualized provided, whatever world there is, or is not, the being of this world, or its non-being, is completely known in some actual infallible awareness, expressive of the essence of the "all-knowing" or "infallible" individual.

So we see that Whitehead's philosophy enables us to synthesize the ancient insight that the existence of deity is of a higher type than all ordinary existence, and is the great anchor which cannot drag, the one unconditional necessity, with the other great insight that reality in the full sense of actuality, even divine actuality, is a surd to all essence, or necessity. So long as philosophers fail to see the difference between a merely existent and an actual entity, it is quite hopeless, I think, to try to clarify such topics as the ontological argument, or the status of Existential judgments with reference to metaphysical issues. We need, in effect, to distinguish "Existentialism" and "actualism." Whitehead is neither an Existentialist nor an essentialist, but an actualist.

If Whitehead preserves a necessity, or absolute security, of existence for God, he also gives a striking interpretation for certain other traditional divine attributes. When, for example, he says that love, which is imperfect in us, is perfect in God, what does he mean? I should say, he means about what he says. Every divine experience expresses a cherishing without stint or reserve of the qualities of all actual lives; for any such reserve would mean fallibility, would mean shutting out from divine attention some real experience somewhere. With us men, sympathy always has reservations. I feel (sometimes, and more or less) how my friends feel, but how those I dislike or find tedious may feel I care little to know, and may be at pains not to know. God dislikes none in this sense and finds none tedious. Is this not the very best of what we call love?

There are, however, those who seem to mean by love an unlimited willingness to accord to the loved one whatever importance in the scheme of things this loved one desires or imagines is appropriate. Thus, if some of us (not all!) imagine it would be appropriate or desirable that our individual life-histories should be endlessly prolonged beyond the grave, then either God loves us not, or he will secure the prolongation. It seems clear that this is a *non sequitur*. I for one incline to view such prolongation as undesirable and inappropriate. But apart from that, do we admit we are unloving every time we veto the desires of our children or our friends? The more friends we have the more certain it is that they will have mutually conflicting desires that cannot all be satisfied, so that choice is unavoidable. Love, in any admirable sense, does not mean endorsing every purpose of another, but rather, taking seriously every feeling and experience of another, in the sense of entering into it, learning its flavor, rather than turning away from it as merely irrelevant or impertinent. As a result of such sympathetic participation, we shall, of course, endorse (with whatever qualifications) many of the purposes of the other, but if we simply endorsed all, we should not be a different person from the other, and certainly not a superior one. Defects of human loving are not in the refusal to accept others' valuations as valid, but in the willful suppression of (or innocent incompetence for appreciating) some part of the evidence to which they appeal. We often refuse to allow our blind spots as to values to be cured by others, or we are unable to have them cured. It is quite another matter to ask us to adopt the blind spots of others as our own!

It may also be asked, is Whitehead's God "righteous"? Does this mean, is God, a dispenser of rewards and punishments that exactly fit the crime, or the good deed, in each case? It is perhaps sufficient to reply that no one knows what this fitness means, and that every theologian (I suppose) has so diluted such "justice" with "mercy" that one cannot tell what in the end it all comes to. But also, it may be said that the whole legal machinery of punishment and compensation is political, not ethical, a defense of minimal social order, and nothing more. The doctrine of heaven and hell is transcendentalized politics, not transcendentalized ethics. There is no truly ethical need for proportional compensation. He who wills good to others for their own sake cannot at the same time find the justification of his acts in the prospect of future reward to himself. To really love others is to find reward now in promoting their good. The ethical crudities that have gone under the name of divine righteousness are indeed something to marvel upon.

Here Whitehead's concept of the self is valuable. A man is a new "actual entity" in every moment or "specious present." True, there is something fixed about his character, but in men—in contrast to God—fixity of character is never absolute, since we can always act "out of character," and in this way develop new characteristics, and since it is arbitrary when, after the fertilized-egg stage, we are said to have first acquired a definite character. But in any case, it is not the fixed character of a man which performs his deeds, nor is it this character that reaps a subsequent reward. It is a momentary self (or sequence of selves) which enacts any given deed, and another later self which experiences the reward. Character, or the man as self-identical, is an abstraction from the sequence of concrete experiences each with its own intrinsic "subject" or "agent." Each such momentary agent reaps the reward of its activity in and with that activity itself, and that is the only reward *this* agent ever can reap! (If it were otherwise, if the very self that has the action should also have its future compensation, then that compensation would not be future but present.) Included in the present satisfaction is whatever sympathy for future members of the personal sequence the present self may feel, and this is "self-interest," but included also is whatever sympathy that self may feel for members of other sequences, human, sub-human, or super-human. This sympathy for other sequences is "altruism." The essential terms of the motivation equation are the momentary concrete acting-and-enjoying self, on the one hand, and whatever future life with which it sympathizes or feels a concern about, on the other. Since all life is embraced in the divine life, the final terms are: present self and God. "Self-interest," as the aim at future advantage for the same sequence of experiences, is merely one important strand in this sympathy of the present self for the future of life and God. To return then to the politico-legal conception of justice, we see that the judge, strictly speaking, punishes one self for acts committed by another. In Whiteheadian terms, the rationale of this can be conceived in at least two ways. For the moment I shall consider only one. Assuming the theory of punishment as deterrence from crime, since there is in normal human experience a dominant strand of sympathy with prospective experiences belonging to the same "personally-ordered" sequence or "linear society," the threatened punishment of later members of such a sequence can very well act as a deterrent upon earlier members, under favorable circumstances—and that is the best that is ever claimed for punishment from the standpoint of its deterrent effect. However, this use of punishment is a means to the end of good behavior which, where possible, is better secured by arousing sympathy not so much for one's own future as for that of others, best of all, for God whose future contains all futures.

It may be thought that the above doctrine destroys the root of responsibility. Can a man repent of misdeeds, if he can always say, "another concrete man it was who performed them, not this concrete actuality which I now am?" But on the contrary, the man is obligated to repentance just to the extent that he has not become a new man in respect to the very tendency to commit the kind of bad act in question. He is a partly new man, true enough; but is the newness relevant to the misdeed? Repentance, with "forgiveness of sins," means, I suggest, being "born anew" in the sense that, in the relevant aspect one is a different man. (This means, of course, a new relation to God, and of God to us.) Past misdeeds are evidence of the need for a partly new character, and until this emerges, and in order that it shall emerge, we should repent. But if repentance has effected its proper result, punishment is out of order, ethically and in so far as the man himself is concerned, though it may have legal and political justification. Thou who hold the other theory of punishment argue that legal "retribution" is at worst better than private revenge, and that human nature demands one or the other. Whether the "guilty man" has been born anew or not, his victims and their friends may have hardened into hatred and rage, and this is a force with which society does have to reckon somehow.

In any case, God's concern, and that of a wise judge, too (or at least, the value of his function), refers to the future, not the past. Even God cannot undo or mitigate the past evil by punishing it; his goal is to work for the optimal future. And moreover, since freedom is inherent in the idea of personality, or even of individuality on any level, God could not manipulate the exact course of events to fit it to a precise scheme of reward and punishment, or to any precise scheme whatsoever. He could not because the idea is an absurdity. The world process is not and could not be a sheer contrivance; it is and could only be a multi-life in an embracing life. Thus, the problem of Job is in a sense a false problem.

The ancient riddle of death and immortality receives in Whitehead's philosophy a new illumination as simple as it is profound. Death is merely a final incident in the fundamental transience of life, as it appears to us when we forget about God. On any day of his life a man has already died, so far as all but a tiny fraction of his past actuality is concerned. A million or so of his experiences have already "perished" into the past. The basic question of permanence concerns not so much the perished men as the perished states or experiences of men, even though still living. For actuality is in experience, and if every experience is impermanent, then all actuality is so. Are the perished experiences reduced to the virtual nothing that we remember of most of them? For the faint memories we have of the past are mere background of the remembering experience, which as an experience is no richer appreciably than most of its predecessors, frequently less so. Is this the entire reality of achieved actuality? No, says Whitehead, for perishing by way of human forgetting may be balanced by a uniquely adequate "objective immortality" in the unforgetting awareness of God. Given this complete preservation, resurrection in any conventional sense seems at best a secondary matter, a problematic luxury, possibly undesirable. (The case for it seems to me to be best presented in the writings of Fechner, A. C. Garnett, and Gustav Strömberg.) Without the immortality of experiences, any heaven would present the same problem of the transience of experiences, which alone are actual values.

It is all very well to say we can live for posterity, for "social immortality." What will posterity ever do with the actual experiences of those dying at Hiroshima, or those going down on a ship? Indeed, how much will posterity know of your experiences, or of mine? Everything, indeed, if posterity includes the divine survivor! He alone is the adequate heir of the true goods of men, their conscious states. To no one other than God can these goods be willed. To him, however, they can be wholly intrusted, with confidence that their true worth will count to the last item.

Concerning the "religious availability of Whitehead's God," (a phrase used by the late Stephen Ely), we may say that if "religion" means the highest form of love between God and man whereby our passing lives achieve everlasting value, then Whitehead's doctrine gives us this far beyond most others. I have one reservation. In a few passages our author does speak as though not all aspects of our experiences could be "saved" for immortality, and A. H. Johnson reports that he unmistakably affirmed this in conversation. However, this seems only to show that Whitehead wavered on the point. For he tells us that the truth is only the way all things are together in the consequent nature, from which it follows that it could not be "true" that something was omitted from the consequent nature. In any case we are free to make this our position, and I know of nothing in Whitehead, save those few passages, which even appears to conflict with it.

We survivors remember bits and echoes of Whitehead's inner life that reached us from time to time. The grace and grandeur of this life many have felt. But let us not imagine that it was but these echoes in us that he was "worth to God." Each man is an addition to the universe, an addition essentially secret. The old mystics saw better than the rationalistic theologians here. "Everlasting life" is what we have at this moment in the heart of deity.

INDEX